Praise for
His Rules

"*His Rules* is de rigueur for any single with a sincere desire to find the 'special sauce' mate God has for them."

—RONN ELMORE, Psy.d, author of *Transforming Your Relationships: An Action Plan for Love that Lasts* (with T.D. Jakes)

"*His Rules* is an amazingly biblical guidebook with practical and relevant encouragement for all singles. Our single sons will all get a copy!"

—PAM AND BILL FARREL, authors of *Men are like Waffles, Women are like Spaghetti* and *Why Men and Women Act the Way They Do!*

"Instead of telling singles how—or not—to date, Burge and Toussaint tell singles how to prepare themselves for the spouse God intends them to have and what to do once they think that person has been found. Their insightful questions and activities help singles delve deep into their own expectations and misconceptions about marriage and lead them toward healthy relationships with the Lord and with their future partner. Christian singles who find their own methods ineffective, as they often are, will be relieved to read this book and find a road map to guide them to and through one of the most important decisions of their lives."

—ALISON STROBEL, author of *Worlds Collide*

"Christopher and Pamela have written a must-read book for Christian singles longing for a soul mate. Each chapter systematically dismantles the fantasies, untruths, and faulty thinking that undermine a successful search for a mate and a successful marriage. *His Rules* equips readers with insights and skills that force them to dig deep within their own souls to prepare themselves for a God-honoring marriage—long before anyone is even in the picture."

—CHERYL GREEN, author of *World Wide Search: The Savvy Christian's Guide to Online Dating*

HIS
RULES

God's Practical Road Map for Becoming
and Attracting Mr. or Mrs. Right

by Christopher L. Burge
& Pamela Toussaint

WATERBROOK
PRESS

His Rules
Published by WaterBrook Press
12265 Oracle Boulevard, Suite 200
Colorado Springs, Colorado 80921

Library of Congress Cataloging-in-Publication Data
Burge, Christopher L.
     His rules : God's practical road map for becoming and attracting Mr. or Mrs. Right / Christopher L. Burge and Pamela Toussaint.— 1st ed.
          p. cm.
     Includes bibliographical references.
     ISBN 1-57856-958-3
     1. Mate selection—Religious aspects—Christianity. 2. Marriage—Religious aspects—Christianity. I. Toussaint, Pamela. II. Title.
     BV835.B87 2005
     248.8′4—dc22
                                                                   2004017794

CONTENTS

PHASE ONE: GET DIESELED

Phase Two: Get Smart

Phase Three: Get Together

ACKNOWLEDGMENTS

Sanctify yourselves, and ye shall be holy.

—LEVITICUS 11:44, KJV

Thanks to my heavenly Dad, my earthly parents, and all my pastors: Pete Scazzero, A. R. Bernard, and Donnie McClurkin, for exampling what it means to be holy, each in your own way, each at the right time.

—Pamela

Thank you, Mom and Dad, for your uncompromising commitment to the things of God. And to my brothers, Daryl and Gregg; and Roxanne for her unwavering support throughout this project. Finally, thanks to the Bible study, for giving me the privilege of sharing the things of God with you on a weekly basis.

—Chris

Many thanks to our supportive publishers, Don Pape and Steve Cobb; our agent, Claudia Cross; our editor, Liz Heaney; and our wise friends and associates, Janet Hill and Sonya White.

—Pamela and Chris

GET DIESELED

In today's divorce-ridden society, it's clear that most of us are entering marriage without enough gas for the trip. We must do the hard work beforehand in order to enter and sustain healthy, thriving marriages. Period. Many of us look good on the outside but are entering relationships malnourished. Only God can give us the Wheaties we need on the inside so we can make our relationships work. Let's deepen our commitment to Him, build up our spirit, and cleanse our soul in preparation for a mate.

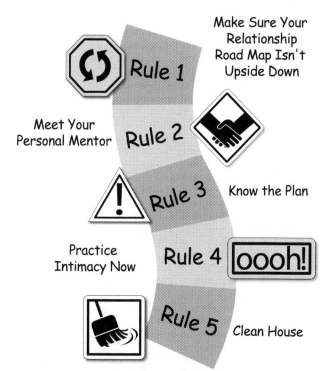

Make Sure Your Relationship Road Map Isn't Upside Down — Rule 1

Meet Your Personal Mentor — Rule 2

Rule 3 — Know the Plan

Practice Intimacy Now — Rule 4 — oooh!

Rule 5 — Clean House

Make Sure Your Relationship Road Map Isn't Upside Down

You have been wandering around
in this hill country long enough;
turn northward.

—Deuteronomy 2:3, NLT

Whenever I (Chris) give workshops on relationships, presenting a biblical view of what to expect in marriage, giddy couples often tell me, "Chris, this teaching was really great, but we just know our marriage will be different."

Many singles travel down Relationship Road, clutching the same dog-eared, upside-down map that has led us to be lost, hurt, and hungry the last fifty times we used it. No wonder we keep engaging in dissatisfying, dead-end relationships. We have bought into marriage myths that need to be exposed and replaced with truth.

Few institutions in our society are under as much attack as the family—particularly the Christian family. This is why we labored to produce this book for you. Why is the family Satan's main place of attack? Because he can get a lot of bang for his buck. If a husband

and wife bicker constantly, lie to one another, or engage in extra-marital affairs, he smiles because he knows the devastation will reverberate to the children and grandchildren. He knows that the sins of the fathers will be passed down to the third and fourth generations[seeExod20:5] unless a person seeks the intervention of the Holy Spirit to address generational curses and other family sins. Satan's fine with our being hand-clapping Christians in church, at Bible study, and during choir rehearsal, as long as we are miserable and contentious at home.

Warning!
Marriage may result in loss of freedom,
flexibility, and disposable income.

The book of Luke says, *For which of you, intending to build a tower, sitteth not down first, and counteth the cost, whether he have sufficient to finish it?*[14:28KJV] The majority of us spend much more time planning our five-hour wedding day than we do preparing for how we're going to live under the same roof with another imperfect person for the rest of our lives. This seems foolish when we look at the divorce rate in this country. Would you fly in an airplane if you knew that it had a 50 percent chance of crashing?

Yet every weekend couple after couple trot down the aisle to the altar, never giving much thought to all of this. To these well-meaning couples, everything about marriage is *ideal*—then after the first year they think it's an *ordeal.* And two or three years later they're looking for a *new deal!* This does not have to be the pattern for *you* if you'll address your upside-down ideas about what happens after dum-dum-da-dum and the Hawaiian honeymoon.

Upside-Down Ideas About Marriage

Many singles enter dating and courtship with these misguided views:

- Marriage is a treasure chest containing all the treats and prizes we've waited for—at no cost.
- Marriage will give us a purpose for living.
- Marriage will get us the unconditional love we deserve—forever.
- Marriage will offer us all the sex we need or all the love we need—on demand.
- Marriage will medicate all the pains of singleness and will solve our deepest longings.
- Marriage will provide us with a spouse whose feelings and beliefs will remain healthy and constant throughout our lives together.
- Marriage will grant us a partner who will intuitively understand our deepest hopes and dreams, and will work eagerly alongside us to accomplish them.

None of these ideas about marriage are true, let alone biblical. Just ask a wife you know if she is able to come home and download all the day's thoughts on her husband each evening as he listens attentively. Ask her husband if he's living out all his sexual fantasies with her each night. Ask them if they feel less vulnerable now that they are married. If they say yes to these questions, they're either extraordinary or they're lying.

Think about it. If marriage was indeed the universal elixir for happiness, why aren't we surrounded by euphoric married couples? (No, the people you see kissing on the street don't count.) Christians should be leading the charge in this area, offering examples of marital bliss for us all to see. But can you think of three Christian couples whose marriages you want to emulate? If not, what makes you believe your marriage will be different? It takes considerable effort *before* you enter a relationship, followed by careful guardianship during the stages leading up to engagement, to give your marriage the nourishment it needs to thrive.

If you can admit that your relationship road map is upside down, make the decision now to allow God's voice to become louder than your emotional fantasies or your false expectations. Our goal in this book is to provide you with the most inexpensive premarital course on the planet. By the time we're done, we want you to know for certain that marriage is *not* a tropical destination where you lie in a hammock and gaze at the ocean for the rest of your life. When we get through dating or courtship and say, "I do," we graduate to a different growth process—some of it painful, but all of it rewarding for those whose marriage road map is right-side up.

Right-Side-Up Views About Marriage

First Be the Right Person, Then Pray for the Right Person

The first part of this book talks about *you* and who you need to be in order to enjoy and be ready for lifelong love. Focus on developing *your* character and on cultivating the fruit of the Spirit—*love, joy, peace, patience, kindness, goodness, faithfulness, gentleness and self-control*—in your life.[Gal5:22-23NIV] Learn to put God first in *your* life (see Rules 2 and 4). Know what God wants you to do with *your* life (see Rule 3). Work diligently on cleaning *your* house (see Rule 5). Proverbs 27:23 says, *Be diligent to know the state of* your *flocks, and attend to* your *herds.* This book will help you take inventory of the sheep and cows in your life—how are they looking? Please hear this: If you want a fabulous, godly mate, you must *become* a fabulous, godly person first.

One day when I (Pam) was reading Proverbs 31, verse 12 struck me. It reads: *She does him [her husband] good and not evil all the days of her life.* I thought, *That's a no-brainer, right?* Wrong. A wise friend helped me realize that "all the days" started *now*, not just after the wedding! That means my current behavior, attitude, and habits need to pass the "Is this doing him good?" test whether I'm in a relationship or not. As I made improvements with the help of the Holy Spirit, it gave me bold authority in prayer to ask God for my mate. Why? Because I knew that I was becoming Mrs. Special Sauce myself.

Your Relationship with Your Spouse Will Only Be as Strong as Your Fellowship with God

Get this: God will never give you anything—even a spouse—that will replace the need for His presence. Why? Because God wants to be first in your life. The spouse He has planned for you will be a tangible, though fallible, representation of His love for you—an earthly manifestation of *Him*. If you don't know Him and His high-quality brand of love for you, you will not know what to look for in a spouse. Only in His presence can you experience true joy. Marriage will, at times, be more challenging than you can possibly anticipate. Where will you go to find joy in those rough seasons, if not to a God you already know and trust? If you do not have a strong, developed, intimate relationship with God that you can lean on, rather than your own understanding or other false comforts, the challenge will overwhelm you. And if your relationship with God is developed but your mate's is not, picture yourself praying alone, seeking counsel alone, and bearing the weight of the marriage challenges alone. Not pretty.

Invest in your relationship with God now, when you are single, and build a firm foundation for your marriage. We know a married mother of four who spent hours with God almost daily when she was single. The strength she gained from building intimacy with Him undergirds her quiet time with Him today, when she has fewer hours to pray and much more to pray for. Will you be able to say the same? Is there clear evidence in your demeanor and conversation that you have a relationship with God? Are you frequently sharing with others what God is doing in your life? If you asked this question of the person you're dating, what would be his or her answer?

Jesus told the disciples, *No longer do I call you servants...but I have called you friends, for all things that I heard from My Father I have made known to you.*John15:15 There is a twofold illustration here. First, Jesus elevates faithful followers to the status of friend. Friends with God—how cool is that! Second, His statement indicates the depth of relationship He has with the Father. Jesus *hears* from God, meaning He spends time listening. But get this part: He also tells *us* whatever He hears! Do you hear from God regularly? He wants to be totally involved in our lives and to show us those great and inaccessible things about JimBob or LuttieMay that we don't know!seeJer33:3 (Learn how to cultivate an ear to hear Him in Rules 2, 3, and 4.)

Marriage Means Taking Off the Garment Called "I Need" and Putting On the Coat Called "I Give"

The scripture Christians often use to introduce others to the love of Christ is a perfect reminder of this principle: *For God so loved the* *world that He gave…*John3:16 True love seeks to give, to uplift, and to be self-sacrificing. Many of us have been duped into believing that marriage is about getting *our* needs and desires met instead of "laying down our lives" for one another. But God says our spouse is to come second only to Him. This means that husbands need to put their wives before their careers or ministry, and that wives also need to put their husbands before their children, careers, or other relationships. Are you capable of loving someone in this way? Is your character ready to handle that level of giving? Ask yourself the same question about the person you are dating or courting. How does he or she measure up?

Encouraging Word

*You have been wandering around in this hill country long enough; turn northward.*Deut2:3NLT

Are you ready to look "northward" for your relationship rules? What false beliefs about marriage are you afraid to let go of?

You may have read the romantic love story of Ruth and Boaz in the Bible. Both demonstrated that they were able to put the needs of others before their own. Boaz wasn't even looking for a wife, but when Ruth came to work in his field, he was clearly moved by what he had heard about her good character. (And he probably thought she was fine, too!) After her first day at work in the fields, he told her to stay near and offered her his protection. When she asked him why he was being so kind to her, a different-looking foreigner, he said: *I've been told all about what you have done for your mother-in-law since the death of your husband—how you left your father and mother and your homeland and came to live with a people you did not know before.*^{Ruth2:11NIV} Word of Ruth's good character had already been fully reported to Boaz before he even met her. Boaz showed her compassion and sensitivity and sought to provide for her. This is notable since Ruth was a Moabite (from the land of Moab, east of Jerusalem), a race often despised by the Israelites, her new neighbors. Boaz showed honesty and faithfulness when he quickly kept his promise to become Ruth's kinsman-redeemer (*kin* means "family," and *redeemer* means "one who rescues"). This makes Boaz a type or symbol of Christ Himself, who is our rescuer. Ruth is a symbol of the church, which is us. This is a true picture of what a godly union should reflect.

Boaz's actions spelled I-N-T-E-G-R-I-T-Y, a quality often lacking in dating relationships today. If we want to marry someone who gives rather than takes, we need to be sure those we date exhibit that quality—and that we do too. If you're in a relationship now, how does it stack up to this example? Allow the Holy Spirit to prick your heart in your areas of weakness. In Chef Emeril's words, let Him take you "up a notch."

Marriage Means Honoring, Cherishing, and Obeying, Even When Money Is Tight and Your Health Fails

On our wedding day, we stand up in our finest duds in front of all the people we love, and promise to love, honor, and cherish each other—in flush times and cash-poor seasons, when our mate is sexy, fit, and healthy, and when he or she is sick, fat, and cranky. And we agree to do all of this "until death do us part." Teary-eyed, we tell the preacher, "I do." If you read these words and think of how dreamy they sound, read them again, but this time take off your rose-colored glasses.

Illness alone can devour our commitment to a marriage, especially if our idea of "two becoming one" is all candlelight dinners and no morning breath. One couple we know was pushed to the brink just two years into their marriage when a car accident left the wife paralyzed from the waist down. The husband was both supportive and attentive to her considerable needs as a paraplegic, and amazingly, they had two sons, despite her confinement to a wheelchair. But after several years, the pressure of her paralysis and two young children overwhelmed the husband. He got tired of trying and had no resources to draw upon because his spiritual life was underdeveloped. The two divorced "amicably," and he later remarried. She now lives with her mother.

Do you have what it takes to withstand something as devastating as what happened to this couple? Your marriage may never face this much adversity, but your partner would probably like to know that you'd be in for the long haul if it did.

Let's look at how you handle minor inconveniences now. Have you learned to be reasonably content even when life stinks? Do you know how to encourage yourself in God when no one else will? Unless you have the proper spiritual foundation, unforeseen circumstances like this will strain your best natural efforts. Our God has said He will *never leave you nor forsake you.*[Heb13:5] Could you promise that to someone?

Financial hardship can also send a delusional marriage partner packing. Disagreement about finances is known to be one of the top marriage killers. It may not seem romantic to watch how your love interest handles money while you're dating or to discuss how you'll spend the "community chest" after the nuptials, but to do so could save your marriage.

The Alvarezes didn't think they had to talk about mundane things like money when they were courting. Four years after their four-hundred-guest cathedral wedding ceremony, their marriage was a mess. Her dream was to have a nice house by the ocean someday; his goal was to retire at age forty. Fine. One problem—they never discussed these hopes seriously. So she began to work extra hours and

A Godly Marriage

Replace the counterfeit images you have of marriage with the truth of God's Word. The Word doesn't talk specifically about how to date (so neither will we), since there was no such thing in biblical times. For the most part, marriages were either arranged or a man saw a woman he liked, and if she liked him, they got married. The scriptures below, taken together, help paint the best picture we can find of how a godly relationship between a man and a woman should look:

- the story of Rebecca and Isaac[see Gen 24]
- the story of Ruth and Boaz[see Ruth]
- God's comments on divorce and controlling our passions[see Mal 2:15-16]
- principles for male/female relationships and for marriage[see 1Cor 7:1-16,25-40]
- mutual submission in marriage[see Eph 5:21-33]
- characteristics of godly wives and husbands[see 1Pet 3:1-7]

Read and reread these scriptures. Meditate on them day and night until you replace your relationship lies with the truth of God's Word.

squirrel away money in a bank account for their someday-beachfront villa. Meanwhile, disgruntled in his teaching job, he was on the brink of quitting and planned to coast awhile on his wife's salary and their savings until he figured out what he really wanted to do. (If he'd sought the Lord when he was single, he wouldn't be putting his family in this predicament. See Rule 3.) One day, she came home to find a new Jeep parked out front. He had quit his job, emptied the savings account, and single-handedly decided that they should spend that summer seeing America. Needless to say, that was one long trip. The couple entered a trial separation shortly afterward.

This story begs the question: How are *you* at money management? Do you run credit cards to their limits? How does your current love interest handle money? Don't make the same mistake the Alvarezes and millions of other couples make. Be candid about your finances and what your dreams are *before* you walk down the aisle. And expect that money-handling will be one of the challenges you will face together in marriage.

PRINCIPLES, NOT SENTIMENTS

Believe it or not, we've only covered a few of the main issues that can threaten a sentiment-based marriage. What if we added a disabled child, an ailing father-in-law, and pornography or alcohol dependency to the household mix? Would you be able to stand firm under those circumstances? For how long? We have deliberately hit you with some heavy items early on, but they are important things to think about now before you become engaged or married. Remember that a strong marriage is based on principles, not feelings.

That buzz you get in your stomach every time he or she walks by won't keep your marriage together very long. There are no shortcuts to building a happy marriage. There are only His rules—tried, true, and time tested.

So does marriage still sound sexy?

If you're disturbed by what you've read so far, good—you are a success story in the making!

Meet Your Personal Mentor

You shall receive power when
the Holy Spirit has come upon you.

—ACTS 1:8

Your sweetheart, an experienced pilot, surprises you with a helicopter ride one beautiful spring Saturday. It's a clear, blue-sky day, so Sweetie decides to let you fly the helicopter for a while. You enjoy the exhilarating feeling of commandeering a helicopter and soaring to new heights. But while flying at a high altitude, you encounter storm clouds that cause the helicopter to bump and slide. The turbulence forces you to give the controls back to Sweetie. What began as an exciting excursion turns into a rough ride that leaves you humbled but glad you could hand things over to someone who knows exactly what to do.

Most people would gladly give up the controls in the above situation. (A few would indignantly continue to fly the copter until forced into a crash landing—but this is not you!) Yet we resist giving up control of our lives to God. Instead, we clutch our Palm Pilots, filling them with goals to pursue, social appointments to attend, obligations to fulfill, *Oprah* to watch, and so on. Often, our agenda is loaded with genuinely good things. So what's the problem? Well, the

Holy Spirit not only wants to fly our helicopter, He also wants to rock our world! He is the ultimate Relationship Counselor. But, gentleman that He is, He'll only assume the role of Personal Mentor in our lives if we invite Him to do so.

And most of us don't.

In his groundbreaking workbook *Experiencing God,* Henry Blackaby asks a probing question: "Suppose you had planned to go fishing or watch Monday night football or go to the shopping mall. Then God confronts you with an opportunity to join Him in something He wants to do. What would you do?"[1] In brief, the possible answers include:

1. Finish my plans, then see if I can fit God's in.
2. Assume that it wasn't God asking.
3. Try to do both.
4. Adjust my plan to God's plan.

Most of us know that number four represents the right answer, but is that really what we do? It can make all the difference, particularly when it comes to our love life.

What Can He Do for You?

Jesus told us that the Holy Spirit's presence in our lives would bring us power.[seeActs1:8] Paul said that the same power that raised Christ from the dead also lives in us to guide us into all truth.[seeJohn16:13] We need His guidance to make right choices about whom to date or court and how to handle ourselves within the relationship.

After Jesus's death and resurrection, He told the disciples that He was going back to the Father and that the Holy Spirit would come and take on the teaching and mentoring role that He had played in their lives. In other words, we have a person of the Godhead, the Holy Spirit, whose specific task is to be our Personal Mentor (PM for short). Jesus knew that we would need the Holy Spirit's help to understand how to live out our Christian faith. We did not receive a brain dump of all we need to know to live a fruitful, God-honoring life on the day we invited Him into our heart. God's revelation of His will is progressive. We will still be learning new things about Him when we're eighty.

Great, you say, but what does that mean for me now?

It means you have a powerful Partner, Mentor, and Relationship Counselor who is always accessible to you. Jesus told His disciples, *If you love me, obey me; and I will ask the Father and he will give you another Comforter, and he will never leave you.*John14:15-16TLB The Holy Spirit will always be there to comfort you, but the Amplified Bible translation of the same set of verses teaches us that He is also our Counselor, Helper, Intercessor, Advocate, Strengthener, and Standby. Here are some ways He functions in those roles:

- *Comforter.* He comforts us when we are feeling sad, lonely, unhappy, hurt, or confused.
- *Counselor.* He advises us, especially when we are facing tough decisions.
- *Helper.* He helps us in our everyday tasks.
- *Intercessor.* He acts as our go-between, mediating between us and God the Father, just as Jesus does.seeHeb7:25
- *Advocate.* He pleads our case to the Father like a top-notch lawyer.
- *Strengthener.* He provides His strength to us when we are tired.

- *Standby.* He is always available to us; He is reliable, especially in emergencies.

The primary ministry of our Personal Mentor (PM) is *apokalupsis*[2] or "uncovering truth for us." Jesus said that the Holy Spirit would *guide you into all the truth* and *tell you things to come.*[John 16:13] That means He enables us to be discerning about the other people in our lives, including our romantic interests. He unveils or pulls back the curtains in our minds and hearts, giving us knowledge, understanding, and guidance that we can't get anywhere else. Left on our own, we are apt to deceive ourselves and make excuses for our own immature behavior. Our PM can give us spiritual eyes to see things about Beautiful Betty or Henry Hottie that will either confirm that they are a good choice for us or that will save us from a nightmare.

But that's not all the Holy Spirit does—there's more. He also shows us ourselves in all our naked glory and splendor.

ADJUST AND REPAIR
YOUR INNER SELF-PORTRAIT

Have you ever noticed the eager look on the face of new parents when they pull out their wallets to show off new pictures of Junior? You see Junior in his jammies…Junior on his first day of pre-K…Junior spitting up peas. The parents don't much care what effect it's having on you; they are thrilled to show off their child's great accomplishments. That's just how your PM feels about you! He will always speak to your greatness and your potential, even when He is convicting you about some area of your character that needs to change.

Knowing how He delights in us makes it easier to take Him up on His offer to help us with a Spirit-led self-exam. He can enable us to take an honest look at both our strengths and our weaknesses and can show us where we need to make changes so that our inner portrait matches His view of us. If we want a fabulous marriage, we will take Him up on His offer to help us become the spouse He made us to be.

If you were having dinner with someone you had a romantic interest in, and he or she happened to ask to see a snapshot of your *internal* portrait—that means you minus the Gucci pumps, the Gold's Gym abs, or the Super-Christian facade—would you rush to pull it out? Would you pull it out at all? Or would you change the subject and motion for the dinner check? As the unveiler, our PM wants to show *us* to *us* first, for our own good, before we get into a serious relationship with someone.

Very often, our inner self-portrait needs a lot of work in order to reflect how God views us. A poor self-image and low self-esteem cause havoc in a marriage and often result in a codependent relationship, which is far from God's best plan. Great marriages require that both spouses exemplify godly character.

Many of us want mates (*now*, please!), but few singles have done the inner work required to be a godly, whole partner. We're convinced that the lack of inner preparation for marriage is a huge part of this country's high divorce rate. So when you pray, "Please, Lord, I need my mate!" know that He will first show you yourself and prompt you to make changes that will make *you* a suitable spouse. You have the choice to follow through with His program for you or to languish in the false comfort of your dysfunction. The program can be long or short, depending on your diligence.

Remember, the Father delights in you. He woos you daily. If you've made a commitment to Him, you are *accepted in the Beloved.*[Eph1:6] That is your position as part of the finished work of Christ on the cross. You are already in the clique, so to speak, and because of that you qualify for the awesome kingdom privilege of having the Holy Spirit at your disposal. He speaks to you because you belong to Him.[seeJohn10:27] Don't let any well-meaning yet unenlightened friends convince you otherwise. Our PM is relentless about getting us to agree with how fearfully and wonderfully we are made and is always seeking to exchange our inner self-portrait with the one Jesus sees.

Peruse the scriptures at the end of this chapter to gain a more correct understanding of how God sees you. Engrave them on your heart. Always know that you are a son or daughter of the King of kings, and that He is not a high priest that is unsympathetic to our humanness.[seeHeb4:15] He came to earth just to be with us. He experienced every possible temptation yet did not sin. He has more than earned your ear, so give Him some talk time.

The quicker we sign up and submit to the changes He wants to make, the quicker we see results. If you listen to your Personal Mentor, He will immediately go to work on you and in you. Not only is He a proud parent who is totally in love with you, but He also wants you to be a fit partner for the work *God prepared in advance for [you] to do.*[Eph2:10NIV] He wants to use your desires, gifts, and abilities, appropriately fitted to your mate's, to share the love of God and the message of salvation. But He cannot work powerfully *through* you until you have given Him the chance to work deeply *in* you. That's why, even though every believer has access to the Holy Spirit, not all Christians experience the many benefits He has to offer. To turn this around, we need to be open to receiving Him, then get quiet, listen, and be willing to submit to what He says.

GET QUIET AND LISTEN

When you're ready to watch a movie at home, you gather all the things you need to make the event enjoyable and comfortable: the big-screen television, the gourmet popcorn, the ten-thousand-calorie pizza, and the oversized chairs. In a similar fashion, when you want to have a serious talk with someone, you're likely to choose a quiet place where you won't be distracted, and you might even bring notes to make sure you talk coherently about whatever is on your mind.

It works the same way to cultivate your relationship with the Holy Spirit. The time you spend with Him is the most important meeting of your entire day, so do what is needed to make it successful. You need commitment in getting to know Him, consistency in meeting with Him, and honesty in talking to Him. Take time out of every day to wait in His presence, compliment Him, thank Him, ask Him questions, and wait for His answers. Keep doing it until your time together becomes a habit that you just can't live without.

Encouraging Word
You hear from Him because you belong to Him. seeJohn10:27

**Do you believe this? Examine any issues you may have
with this statement and take them to God.**

Establish an ongoing dialogue with God; let your PM speak to you in your quiet times and throughout the day. Remember that God

wants to talk to us; we do not have to assault the throne to get Him
to chat. The book of Revelation tells us that He stands at the door and
knocks, like a polite houseguest.[seeRev3:20] He will not barge into our
busy lives, break down the door, grab us by the shoulders, and make
us listen to Him. So if we want to hear Him, we have to pay attention and listen carefully. James tells us we should be *swift to hear, slow
to speak.*[1:19] God speaks in *a still small voice.*[1Kings19:12] But with persis-
tence and practice, we can strengthen our listening skills. (Good listening skills will also come in handy with your future mate, as we
discuss in Rule 15.)

If you are not sure that you can recognize or hear God's still
small voice, get to know Him better and learn of Him until you
are.[seeMatt11:29] Here are some specific ways you can strengthen your
relationship with God:

- *Get your praise on.* Praise is when you reach up to kiss God
  and thank Him for who He is and what He's done for you.
  It is the precursor to worship, which is a deeper intimacy
  with Him. In the University of praising God, where do
  you stand? Will you graduate cum laude: praising Him
  on Sunday mornings and when everything in your life is
  spiffy? Magna cum laude: praising Him even when things
  are just so-so? Or summa cum laude: able to praise Him
  though life's killing you (like the apostle Paul in the dun-
  geon[seeActs16:25-27])? Perhaps you're not close to graduating
  yet. That's okay; get going today! The level of your praise
  will reveal the level of your relationship with God.

- *Make true confessions.* Jesus taught us to pray and ask His forgiveness for our ugly actions each day and to pray for those
  who hurt us each day. Don't even think about asking Him for

something if you are harboring unconfessed sins or grudges. Confess sins of omission (things you didn't do, but should have) and commission (things you did do, but shouldn't have).

• *Make His Book your favorite book.* My (Chris's) relationship with God deepened when I committed to reading through the entire Bible, book by book. (We call it our Sixty-Six-Book Love Letter.) I chose a version of the Bible I knew I could understand easily, *The Living Bible* translation, and as a naturally early riser, I was up at dawn rummaging through it.

On the other hand, I (Pam) use several translations and a concordance when I'm reading the Bible so I can better capture the nuances and principles. I highlight in yellow any scriptures that God brings alive to me, and then I memorize them. You might need another approach entirely—find your own groove. We pray the Bible becomes the best-read Book on your bookshelf!

Suggestion: Read a psalm in the morning and a chapter of either the Old Testament or the New at night—or vice versa if you have more time in the morning. This strategy breaks the text down into bite-sized morsels you can chew on without cracking your teeth. After a while, you'll end up reading much more than you planned. (Fortunately, you can't OD on God's Word!)

• *Have fireside chats.* During your time with God, thank Him and make requests of Him based on what He just showed you in the Word. Talk about whatever He brings up in your spirit. God will often use a scripture you've read to tell you something personal (that's called *rhema*). Conclude your time with more thanks.

If your PM tells you something that you need to do during your quiet time, submit to it.

Cultivate Submission

Submit has become a dirty word both inside and outside of church circles due to its misuse. We hope that it will enjoy a revival as it is critical to our relationship with God and to our ability to maintain a lifelong love relationship. Remember, Jesus was able to submit to the torture of dying on the cross because of the Holy Spirit's power. He lives in us and gives us that same power.

Submission is the residue of true love. When we know that God loves us unconditionally and totally, we won't find submission to Him difficult. (Love is the quality that's often missing in marriages where there's "trouble with submission.") The prefix *sub* means to "come under." A subway runs under the ground, a subcutaneous wound is one that is under the skin, and so on. Webster says that *submit* means "to yield to governance or authority." We tap into the power of our PM when we submit to His authority and guidance in our life. It's essential to cultivate this ability to yield to the Holy Spirit if we want to grow spiritually—and to have a healthy relationship with Mr. or Mrs. Right.

Here are some examples of things your PM might ask you to submit to:

- Stop telling "little white lies."
- Keep your mouth shut when you really want to give someone a piece of your mind.
- Call someone with whom you are estranged and be the one to restart communication.

- Attend a midweek Bible study, even though you are a faithful Sunday church attendee and are tired after work.
- Get involved in church activities and submit to someone (who you might not feel is as smart as you are).
- Quit watching a certain television show or attending a particular social gathering, even though it may not be explicitly immoral.

Marriage provides you with a constant traveling mirror and a person to hold it up (sometimes when we least want to see ourselves). The marriage union presents a controlled environment in which God can use your mate to help you develop character. But a mate cannot, should not, and will never be your savior—only God can play this role in your life effectively. People with savior complexes get tired because they are operating in their own limited strength. Your PM is all-powerful and never tires. Submit to Him now so that you can enter into marriage whole. (If you need the Savior, turn to the Lordship Prayer on page 69.

If we don't submit to the work of our PM, our inner portrait will remain marred, and we will subconsciously attract the type of person our damaged self-portrait says we deserve. (Sadly, this is not even the real you; it's just the you that you refused to submit for cleaning.) Don't let this happen. It takes years to recover from the pain of a broken marriage, and you don't have that kind of time, right? Right!

When you allow your PM to guide you, your life will become characterized by *the peace of God, which surpasses all understanding.*Phil4:7 You will experience a freedom from any anxiety you may have had. (Although the issue that was a catalyst for the anxiety may not change immediately or at all, *you* will change). God's peace surpasses any sight, sense, or circumstance you are facing—it goes beyond our natural understanding. Armed with this deep-down peace, you can trust God about your future, even when the clock is ticking and no one you like is giving you the time of day…yet.

Kill the "Maybe I's"

Perhaps as you read this you're thinking:

- *Maybe I just don't have the time for this process; I need to cut to the chase.*
- *Maybe I am not good enough to have a relationship with God.*
- *Maybe I won't hear anything from God.*
- *Maybe I am not doing it right.*
- *Maybe I deserve the mess I'm in anyway.*

If any of these thoughts resonate with you, we urge you to kill them right now. First of all, God is never in a mad rush. He wants things done right, for our own benefit. He will show you that you do have the time. In fact, you don't have time *not* to have the time with Him! Satan always drives from behind and is always negative and condemning. God always draws from the front and is always positive and encouraging, even when He chastises.

You will never regret the time you spend getting to know your PM. He will be your Friend and Relationship Counselor for life.

Know the Plan

"I know the plans I have for you,"
declares the LORD.

—JEREMIAH 29:11, NIV

Don't leave home without it" was the once-popular slogan of the American Express card. We need a similar watchword for our lives. Too many of us make choices without the clarity and peace of knowing God's plan and purpose for us. We enter relationships, make career moves, and grasp at various opportunities only to feel confusion and disappointment as we repeat patterns of limited promise. If you are waiting for your future mate to get you on the road to discovering your gifts, the chances are high that you'll end up with a partner whose vision is vastly different from your own. To avoid this, you need to work to discover your purpose now, while you are still single.

God has designed a heavenly assignment for each of us, including you. Just as the lilies of the field are imprinted with God's unique design, so He has imprinted your heart with eternity and your life with His purpose. He has put you into this time and this place for a special reason. Don't wander aimlessly through life, grasping at false goals and aspirations and failing to complete the assignment that has your name on it. Each day that we live without pursuing God's vision for us, we move a little closer to death—mentally, emotionally, spiritually, and—finally—physically. The book of Proverbs says, *Where there is no vision, the people perish.*[Prov29:18KJV]

Not only must you know your God-given purpose, you also must be able to trust a potential mate's ability to hear and follow the Holy Spirit's leading, as his or her decisions will affect the rest of your life. How can a woman follow a man who has no sense of his divine assignment? How can she help a mate achieve a goal that doesn't exist or isn't from God? On the flip side, what good is it for a man to have a clear sense of what God wants him to do if he's married to a woman who wants no part in it? A man or woman who continually chases after the next million-dollar idea without consulting God will be unstable externally and in turmoil internally. Men in particular feel a constant angst when they feel their "ducks are not lining up." This inner dissatisfaction inevitably leads to relationship troubles.

So if you don't have an idea of what God wants you to do for Him on this earth, you need to spend more time pursuing Him until you do. Here are some fool-proof principles for finding out His plan, starting with the most important step.

TALK TO THE MANUFACTURER FIRST

We must know *whose* we are before we can know what we are here to do. That means doing the things we talked about in the last chapter: getting to know God, spending time talking to Him, and listening for Him to speak to us.

Since God knows the good plans He has for us, why are we dialing up psychic hotlines, checking our horoscopes in the newspaper, or turning on TV psychologists at 2:00 a.m. in order to discover our destiny? Such activity is an affront to the One who created us. The pop culture answer can never compare with God's unique prescription for our individual lives. When we turn to anyone or anything but God to determine our destiny, we're making a dumb and dangerous move. Psalm 1:1 says we are blessed if we stay away from the counsel of those who don't know God. Why would we go anywhere but to the Manufacturer to ask for instructions on how to make our lives work? We were conceived, fashioned, and produced by God. He wrote your owner's manual; now read it! *Selah.*

DISCOVER, DON'T DECIDE

Spending the time with God, asking Him to reveal His plan and purpose for your life, will yield significantly different results from simply deciding what *you* want to do, apart from Him. Yet many of us do exactly that; we determine what we want, then ask Him to bless our plan. As the author and finisher, God is not obligated to bless life directions He did not establish.[seeHeb12:2]

God has given us the Holy Spirit so we can know the truth, and He says that if we lack wisdom, all we have to do is ask—*Him.*[seeJames1:5] If you ask your PM, He will help you discover God's vision for your life. Vision comes from heaven down, not vice versa.[seeActs26:19] It should not come from your own finite mind.

The same is true when it comes to deciding whom to marry. We must be sure that we are choosing a mate who, as far as we can discern, is in line with God's purpose for us. (That's why we need to know our God-given purpose before we seriously consider marriage.) Do not pursue someone because he or she looks good (or sounds good) and then cry out to God later because that person does not fit into His vision for you. Instead, take time now to discover God's destiny for you, then go on to discover His mate for you.

TRUST THAT HE'S EQUIPPED YOU

One reason some people don't seek God's purpose for their lives is that they are afraid to put themselves, and more specifically their precious career plans, into His hands. They fear that He will make them go to the outskirts of the jungle, even though they are traumatized when one mosquito comes near them. They are sure that if they ask Him what they should do with their lives, whatever He has in mind will definitely not be fun.

Nothing could be further from the truth.

God is not a killjoy. In fact, He created joy! He knew you before you were even an idea in Mommy and Daddy's heads. Think about it: Why would an all-knowing, loving God call you to an assignment for which you are totally unsuited and uninterested? The job wouldn't get done (at least not very well), and He'd have a miserable ambassador to contend with. Your Father has already equipped you with the talent, resources, and desire that will move you forward in your assignment, despite the obstacles you will face in completing it. He had to or else you would not make it. You already possess both the passion and stamina you need to complete the destiny He has designed for you and to run with the vision He births in you. Ephesians 2:10 says, *For we are His workmanship, created in Christ Jesus for good works, which God prepared* **beforehand** *that we should walk in them.*

Consider these examples of men and women whom God called to do a specific task for Him:

- Paul, one of the greatest evangelists and church planters in Christian history, told the church he planted in Rome that he had a great desire to visit them and that he *made it [his] aim* to preach the gospel to those who had not heard, even in the midst of great adversity.[Rom15:20]

- At the risk of displeasing the king and being put to death, Esther went to him uninvited in hopes of winning his favor and saving her people, the Jews, from execution. She spent time in fasting and prayer, then faced her assignment with courage and determination, exclaiming, *If I perish, I perish!*[Esther4:16] God not only gave her an assignment, He equipped her to do the job. The king was so smitten with Esther that he told her he would grant any request she made, so when she asked him to spare her people, he did!

- Carrying only a slingshot and five small stones, young David had the boldness to mouth off to a giant at the start of his career: *This day the LORD will hand you over to me, and I'll strike you down and cut off your head. Today I will give the carcasses of the Philistine army to the birds of the air and the beasts of the earth.*[1Sam17:46NIV] A few minutes later, David did exactly what he had boasted. God had called him to do something everyone around him thought was impossible and made a simple slingshot into a lethal weapon.

- The prophet Jeremiah shed tears constantly, so heavy was his burden for the Israelites to turn back to God and escape judgment. His assignment consumed him: *His word was in my heart like a burning fire shut up in my bones; I was weary of holding it back, and I could not.*^{Jer20:9} Did you get that? Jeremiah was so determined to fulfill the call of God that he *could not* hold himself back from doing it. That's passion!

Encouraging Word
Jeremiah's vision was in his heart,
like a burning fire shut up in his bones.

What is the thing your heart burns to accomplish
or to help make happen in the world? Your answer
will provide a great start to discovering your destiny.

None of these men or women seemed bored or afraid of their missions, even though they often faced adversity in order to complete the task. As they accomplished their God-given assignments, their gifts brought them before their country's leaders and caused them to prosper beyond their wildest dreams. This principle is still the same two thousand years later. Do all you can to fulfill God's agenda, and He will bless you as a byproduct of your obedience.^{seeMatt6:33}

BE PATIENT AND OPEN

As we pray for God to reveal His plan for us, we need to be patiently open to hearing from Him however and whenever He wants to talk to us. He may answer our prayers for direction through a song, a psalm, a person, a television commercial, a sign on a truck, or even a dream. Make sure your preconceived notions about how God "should" speak don't hinder your hearing.

God recently brought this truth home to a friend of ours. One evening she was praying for God to send her mate. Later that same night, she set a pot of water on the stove and hovered over it, waiting for it to boil. The water seemed to take hours to even simmer. God used that pot of water to speak to her in a *still small voice,*[1Kings19:12] telling her that she needed to stop worrying about her love life and go on and do the things that He had already told her to do to get prepared for a mate. He assured her that if she obeyed Him in the things she knew to do, then He would take care of her—the water *will* boil.

Sometimes God gives people a big-picture vision for their life—such as marriage or a call to ministry or a particular profession; other times He simply reveals one small part of His vision.

Take Joseph as an example. When he was young, he had a couple of symbolic dreams that indicated he would rule over people, but he wasn't given side notes about when or how all this would happen. Then his brothers sold him into slavery. Joseph spent thirteen years as a servant in a foreign country, only to go to prison for several more years. Nice. Though it certainly must have seemed to him that he had misunderstood God, God was strengthening Joseph's character, teaching him to stand up under pressure. While Joseph was still in prison, God used his ability to interpret dreams to bring him into the presence of Pharaoh, who rewarded Joseph by making him second in command over the whole region. Subsequently, as a ruler in Egypt, he had a lot of pressure to deal with, but his previous experiences had served to equip him for this role.

Know that God is concerned with character readiness when it comes to His plan for us. Most of the time, when He asks us to wait before He reveals our destiny, it's because He wants us to grow and develop into people who can withstand adversity. If you have been seeking Him, yet still don't have a clue about your destiny, perhaps it's because you haven't acted on the things He's already revealed to you. Maybe He's asked you to work on a character weakness or to stop putting your desire for a spouse above your desire for Him. Perhaps He has nudged you to get an accountability partner, to read a certain book on relationships, to get involved in a ministry or service project through your church, or to do something that seems totally unrelated to your destiny (such as reconciling with that sister you haven't talked to in years). Don't brush these things off as insignificant—do them.

Write Down the Plan

As God begins to reveal bits and pieces of His plan for you, consider writing it in a journal. As you add to it over time, you'll begin to develop a clear picture of what He wants you to accomplish for the kingdom. This is crucial because when the challenges of life make you question if you are doing what God wants, you will need something other than your circumstances to confirm it. If you don't have a documented description, the vision God has given you may not seem real in light of your current problems or past errors.

We've both seen the benefits of doing this. I (Chris) have a list of things that I believe God wants me to do before I die. This list has helped me know whether a particular direction or action I'm considering is on God's radar screen. One of the things on the list is writing books, so when the opportunity came along for me to cowrite this book, I prayerfully pursued it, confident that it fit into the destiny that God has for me.

I (Pam) have known that I was to be a writer since I was in the sixth grade and have successfully pursued that vocation. But a few years ago, as I sought to find out what else God wanted me to accomplish, He showed me that I needed to develop hidden talents in two very different areas—cooking and counseling, both of which brought me a lot of joy. I wrote in my journal that I felt God was calling me to take these talents to a new level, and I began to seek training in both areas. Today, my mom and I run a catering business and plan to open a café. We found out that feeding people well is a ministry too! As I listened to the voice of my PM wooing me, I made myself available to God to bless, exhort, and pray for people in my sphere of influence. My pastor saw my potential and assigned me to the ministry team at my church. When I stepped out in faith and pursued these hidden gifts, God made a way for me to pursue His destiny for my life.

If you want to discover God's plan for your life, start by writing down the answers to these twelve questions:

1. What did you do for fun when you were a child? What came easy to you?
2. What do you do that causes people to say, "You're so good at that!"
3. What about the world most excites you? What angers you about the world?
4. What are the characteristics of the life you most envy?
5. What would you be doing if you were ten times bolder?
6. How do you usually spend a free afternoon?

Living It Out: Chris's Story

I was a thirty-two-year-old Wall Street salesman when God told me I would attend Bible school one day. I wrote this down in my journal and filed it under "Things to Do Twenty Years from Now." Little did I know that God's plan to bring that to pass in my life was already in the works before the ink was dry! I was entering the tenth year of a job I loved and excelled at. I was comfortable financially and sure I would be a "lifer" on The Street, as New Yorkers call Wall Street. I attended all the right functions with all the right people in the finance world. I was even highlighted in our company brochure and featured in *Black Enterprise* magazine.

I had it made. But all of a sudden I felt this tug on my heart that it was time to leave. *Leave?* I thought. *That's crazy! Go to Bible school now? No way.* But I quickly saw I had lost zeal for the job I had loved. Half the time I couldn't concentrate and was disinterested. I guess I could have rebelled or been anxious about the future, but I could see that God was taking away my comforts in order to boot me out of the nest. I already knew that going to Bible school was His plan for me; I just hadn't realized the time was now. I knew that I always had peace whenever I followed the Holy Spirit's leading, and I knew how bad I felt when I didn't. So I adjusted my schedule to His and plunged ahead.

Less than three months later, I turned in my resignation, sublet my Manhattan apartment, packed up, and headed West—for Oklahoma, no less! When I landed in the quiet Tulsa International Airport, I thought I had truly lost my mind. What a change from bustling New York! I asked the Lord if this was some sort of cosmic joke. God assured me it wasn't. I just had to trust. I thought about Jeremiah 29:11. The truth that God knows the plans He has for us was unfolding before my eyes.

Three years later I had experienced the greatest seasons of my life in that Oklahoma town. I grew exponentially in the things of God. With fewer distractions, I spent concentrated time in His presence and engaged in rigorous Bible study, sitting under great teaching on a daily basis. My relationship with the Lord and my understanding of God's Word and His character began to deepen, and His call on my life began to crystallize. When I took that step out of my comfort zone—away from my plan for myself and my future—and moved toward the place I believed God was leading me, He unlocked everything else. As I moved, He gave me more clarity about additional steps.

One day, I saw an illustration in a book that made a lot of sense to me and spurred me on. It was called the "corridor principle": Life can sometimes be like a dark corridor, and as you walk down it, you see doors of opportunity you never would have glimpsed if you'd stayed in the lobby. As a result of walking down my faith corridor, I have a clarity that goes beyond words about why I am on the earth. I experience more fulfillment as I pour out my gifts on others through a weekly, large-group Bible study than I ever did working on The Street. I have the privilege of being a catalyst for hundreds of mostly single thirty-somethings, to be enlightened, encouraged, and changed to the glory of God.

Who could ask for anything more?

7. What can you not imagine living without?

8. If you could add just one accomplishment to your life, what would it be?

9. What are your hidden talents? How does your work give you the opportunity to express those talents?

10. When you daydream, what do you think about most?

11. What do you want to learn more about?

12. What touches your emotions more than anything else?

Don't Get Sidetracked

Once God has spoken to you about His plan for you, don't get off track. Even when we have a glimpse of our purpose on this earth, that vision can get lost in the voices of our society and the constraints of cultural traditions. Our families and friends can be the first ones to distract us from fulfilling our God-given identity and purpose. They may say: "You're too young," "You're too old," "You're the wrong color or nationality," "You're not smart enough," "You have no money," and so on.

For example, Joseph desires to leave his corporate job to launch a youth ministry but struggles because he knows that his high-achieving family and friends would freak out. Sofia feels called by God to be an artist, but her father, who sacrificed a great deal for their family, insists that she have three letters after her name (and MFA wasn't on his list). Vince, who is in his thirties, never finished college and took a blue-collar job only to realize—a wife and two toddlers later—that he's called to be a writer. He's frustrated and scared that his lack of education, as well as his financial and familial obligations, will keep him from fulfilling his God-given dream. Like many of us, his heart is full of the

Enemy's plan stoppers, which often begin with, *If only I hadn't...* Is yours? If so, your Personal Mentor has the antidote.

As we said in Rule 2, your PM's voice must become so loud that it mutes any contrary voices in your life. If you don't have a deep-down

Plan Stoppers: Self-talk from our heritage that halts the plan of God in our lives.

If only I hadn't...

- *had the parents I have;*
- *grown up in the neighborhood, city, or country I did;*
- *quit school;*
- *become a single parent;*
- *followed my peers into dead-end jobs.*

Antidotes: Self-talk from our spiritual heritage that lets loose the plan of God in our lives.

I know...

- *I was knit together with tremendous care and marvelous complexity;* seePs139:13
- *I am thought of continuously by my heavenly Father;* seeIsa55:8-11
- *a great price was paid for me to be in the world as a child of God;* see1Cor6:20
- *I can do all things through Christ who strengthens me;* Phil4:13
- *my true heritage is in Christ Jesus and it is glorious.* see1Pet.2:9

sense of peace and satisfaction about what you are hearing, the plan may not be from God. If you are sincerely meditating on who God says you are, spending time in the Word until it changes how you think, and submitting to your PM day by day, you are far less likely to be misled or deceived. Again, let peace be the final authority in all you hear.[seeCol3:15]

Think of it this way: The Bible is our instruction manual and our PM is the toll-free number God has provided for tech support. The first thing the agent on the support line will ask is, "Did you read the manual?" So make sure that whatever you think He is saying to you lines up with the written Word of God. Obviously, the Bible will not say, "Julie should go to medical school in Baltimore." But God will not reveal a plan to you that violates any of His laws or principles. Don't kid yourself by twisting and mixing truth with untruth in order to justify your own aims.

Here's one final scenario: Let's say you grab hold of the scripture that says God wants you to *prosper in all things and be in health, just as your soul prospers.*[3John1:2] So you decide to pack up and move to a greener, healthier state or country. Never mind that you are leaving behind a dynamic church where you are experiencing tremendous spiritual growth and enjoying good fellowship. You are consumed with being prosperous and healthy, which you've decided will be impossible to accomplish in Smallsville. Watch it. You don't want to be anywhere God isn't. In Exodus 33:12-15, Moses and God were chitchatting when *[Moses] said to Him, "If Your Presence does not go with us, do not bring us up from here."*[v15] It's better to be in a studio apartment eating cereal for dinner *with* God, than on an estate feasting without Him.

Here are some things He will never lead you to do:

- *Create or start something that obviously feeds another person's weakness.* No, you cannot take a job managing a nightclub to fulfill your entrepreneurial gifts. Your great plan to witness to customers doesn't make this wrong decision right, nor does the argument that the increased pay will enable you to tithe more to your church. No! If you have an opportunity to *buy* a nightclub and turn it into a God-honoring establishment, that plan is in line with Scripture.

- *Allow something to draw you further away from His presence.* No, He would never lead you to start a business that keeps you out of church service, so don't try to justify it by giving Holy Spirit Cruises for groups who want to go sailing only on Sundays.

- *Compromise your marriage vows or your responsibilities as a parent in order to fulfill His plan for your life.* No, you don't leave your toddler with your mother in another state so you can go get your master's degree!

- *Follow a plan that necessitates your compromising His value system in order to be successful* (such as lying, cheating, or violating established moral and ethical conduct).

- *Follow a plan you can accomplish without Him.* If you can do it on your own, He is not in it!

BECOME GOD'S MIDWIFE

As you're waiting to discover your life purpose and destiny, be willing to let God use you to bring about His purposes in the world and in other people. Shiphrah and Puah, two obscure but important Egyptian midwives from the book of Exodus, provide excellent examples of how we can serve others while we wait patiently for God. Their job was to make something great happen for someone else, to help other women give birth. When crazy Pharaoh issued a decree for the murder of all boys born to Hebrew women, these midwives refused to obey because they feared God.^{seeExod1:17} Instead, they let the male babies they delivered live. As a result of their courage and obedience, God blessed them and provided them with children of their own (implying that they may have been barren or unmarried).

What's our point? Simply this: Even if you have yet to identify God's plan and purpose for your life, don't sit around waiting for Him to write the plan on your bedroom ceiling! Help others give birth to His vision for their lives. Since you are reading this book, we know you dream of being married someday. Don't just sit waiting for that to happen, either. Perhaps you need to get over me, myself, and I.

That was true for me (Pam). A few years ago I was meeting weekly with one of my best friends to pray. We prayed for five people we knew and for ourselves (asking for mates, of course). Well, one fine day, her mate showed up, but mine didn't. In the midst of my friend's joy, I started to feel disappointment and self-pity. But then God challenged me to support her throughout her courtship and engagement (and do it smiling). So I decided to concentrate on doing that well instead of focusing on what I didn't have. I became the engagement lunch-giver, shower-thrower, and best girl at the wedding. As I waited for God to unfold the Pam Plan, I allowed Him to use me to unfold His plan for her. I felt such a sense of His pleasure as I supported my friend, and I know the Word of God says, *For God is not unfair. He will not forget how hard you have worked for him and how you have shown your love to him by caring for other Christians, as you still do.* Heb6:10NLT

When we use our time and talents to serve the body of Christ at large, we also learn to lay down our own desires for something greater than ourselves. God knows you could be doing any number of things instead of serving people: sleeping, working late, chatting on the phone, going to Happy Hour, sleeping some more, and so on. He will honor you for your good choice.

Serving others can help you develop patience, hope, faith, joy, and a peace that even your mind won't understand—all fruits necessary for sustaining lifelong love. Plus, that mate you desire might be serving right alongside you in the children's ministry, youth service, choir, homeless outreach, drama team, intercessors group, or friend's wedding reception. But you'll never know if you don't make yourself available to serve.

As we prepare for lifelong love, we need to be sure we are following the right road map, listening and submitting to the voice of the Holy Spirit, and asking God to show us His plan for our lives. But that's not all. We also need to bone up on our intimacy skills so that we can be prepared to have real intimacy with Mr. or Mrs. Right.

Read on to find out how.

Practice Intimacy Now

Rise up, my love, my fair one, and come away.

—SONG OF SOLOMON 2:10

In a scene from the A. A. Milne classic, *The House at Pooh Corner:* "Piglet sidled up to Pooh from behind.

" 'Pooh!' he whispered.'

" 'Yes, Piglet?'

" 'Nothing,' said Piglet, taking Pooh's paw. 'I just wanted to be sure of you.' "[3]

As any relationship progresses and deepens, we, like Piglet, want to "be sure of" the other person. Yet because we know so little about what real intimacy requires before we get into a relationship, our efforts to be sure often fail. Many couples confess that they got married based on romantic feelings (what we call "the giddies") and then struggled for years to figure out what true intimacy was really about, often at their mate's expense. Intimacy is even more elusive for those of us who grew up in abusive or single-parent homes, where we may not have known what—or who—was a sure thing from one day to the next. But what if we were able to practice intimacy with someone we could be absolutely certain of? Wouldn't that give us a leg up on developing a marvelous marriage?

Relationship experts exhort couples to "learn your mate" and "make a study of him or her" in order to develop oneness and intimacy. Relationships fail because people stop learning about one another. We say, "He changed" or "I just don't know who she is anymore," but that's not really what happened. We focus on being seen but not on seeing the other person, which allows us to imagine that the other person is someone he or she is not. Intimacy begins with a desire for oneness and requires both the willingness to reveal ourselves to the other and the desire to truly know the other.

Jesus invites us into intimacy with Him when He says simply and eloquently, *Learn from Me.*[Matt11:29] We believe that His example of oneness with the Father and the Holy Spirit shows us what intimacy involves and provides us with a blueprint for intimacy in our relationships. We see in the first chapter of Genesis (which means "origin or beginning") that this Awesome Threesome worked as a unit when they decided to create man: *Let **Us** make man in **Our** image.*[Gen1:26] If you've ever been involved in group decision making, you know that kind of unity requires some remarkable cooperation! Indeed, Jesus says He only does what He sees His Father doing and that the Holy Spirit only says what Jesus says.[seeJohn8:38;16:13] The Father only does or says things that bring honor to His Son, and He only acknowledges those who come to Him using His Son's name as a reference.[seeJohn14:9-11] They are all so in love with one another that their harmony is perfect and complete—the Father, Son, and Holy Spirit are always in sync.

Can we hope to achieve that kind of unity in our earthly relationships? Yes! First, Jesus invites us to be part of the tight relationship He has with the Father and the Spirit when we receive Him as Lord. As believers, we become members of that same holy clique.[seeEph1:6] If you aren't in the clique yet, turn to the Lordship Prayer on page 69, close your door, pray, and enter in! (We'll wait for you.)

We were created for intimacy, first with God and then with one another. Any other order is backward and will backfire. So the best way for you to practice intimacy while you're single is to essentially become His spouse first. This means more than receiving Him as your Savior; it means making Him Lord of your life. The two are not the same. Here's the difference: I (Pam) went forward one night at a church service and accepted Christ as my Savior by making a verbal confession of what I believed in my heart. Yet it was years before I gave Him permission to do whatever He wanted with my life. Only then did our relationship of intimacy begin.

When we feel utterly accepted by God because we are holding nothing back from Him, we free ourselves to *be* ourselves in a relationship with someone else. We get there by seeking God's face, longing after Him, and surrendering to Him. A. W. Tozer put it this way:

> The stiff and wooden quality about our religious lives is a
> result of our lack of holy desire. Complacency is a deadly foe
> of all spiritual growth. Acute desire must be present or there
> will be no manifestation of Christ to His people. He waits to
> be wanted. Too bad that with many of us He waits so long,
> so very long, in vain.[4]

So, What's Our Problem?

James 4:8 says that if we draw near to God, He'll draw near to us. That's quite a promise. The Almighty waits for *us* to come closer to Him so that He can woo us, be near us, love us, and provide for us.

Again, when we get to know and love God, we will know how to properly love and be loved by another person.

If longing after God brings results into our lives, why are so few of us seeking intimacy with Him? Perhaps it's because we're comfortable with the sense of control we gain by keeping Him at a safe distance. We let Him come only as far as we want Him to come and then say, "Thanks, I can handle it from here." But such behavior will never result in intimacy.

It has been said that *intimacy* can also be spelled *into-me-see*. Intimacy with God requires that we invite Him to see the Good Me, the Bad Me, and the Very Bad Me. But letting God into the Bad Me and Very Bad Me sections of our hearts will require us to go to a deeper level of trust with Him than we may have known up to this point. Usually, we don't want anyone, especially God, rummaging around in our dirty closets. We aren't sure He'll love us if He sees what we think we've hidden from Him.

This fear of intimacy can be easier to spot in our romantic relationships. See if this pattern rings true in your life: When you first enter a relationship you're excited, in love, and inseparable, headed for the altar. Then suddenly something starts to feel wrong and you slow down, or the other person slows down. It might be because the other person turned out to be a different person up close than he or she seemed on the surface. But if you are like many, it's because the other person was getting too close, and a latent fear of intimacy surfaced, so you backed away, often without knowing the real reason you wanted distance from this person.

Many of us do the same thing in our relationship with God. We are in it for the initial buzz, but not for the long haul. We leave Him out of our decisions unwittingly; we don't even realize we're excluding

Him. But when we do this, it stunts the growth of our intimate relationship with Him, and thus slows our ability to be intimate with Mr. or Mrs. Right when they come along. The more "closets" of our lives that we allow Him into, the more accepted and loved by Him we'll feel, and the more He helps us handle life's hurdles. If we keep certain areas of our lives off limits, we won't have the benefits of true oneness with Him when life gets out of control. It usually takes a circumstance beyond our control or our ability to solve to get us to the place where we are willing to say to God, "Into-me-see."

Additional barriers to cultivating transparency with God include:

- *Unconfessed sin.* This leads to guilt and shame that makes us want to hide from God.

- *Poor self-esteem and insecurity.* When you don't feel good about yourself, it's very hard to believe someone else can love you, especially someone you can't see.

- *Unforgiveness toward God, self, or others.* We often blame God for things that aren't His fault but are a result of our sin or disobedience, or that of others. When we crucify ourselves for mistakes, we are engaging in the highest form of pride. We are saying that Jesus's death on the cross wasn't enough to atone for our error. The Bible says that our prayer lives are hindered when we hold unforgiveness toward others.seeMark11:25-26

- *Mistrust or lack of trust.* When authority figures or loved ones have abused your trust, it can be difficult to trust God.

When we continue to linger behind the barriers that keep intimacy with Him from growing, we dishonor Him and harm ourselves. Furthermore, we set ourselves several steps back on the road to that godly mate.

LETTING GOD IN

Perhaps you're wondering, *I go to church and I pray. Isn't that enough? What else do I have to do to attain this high level of intimacy with God?* While going to church and praying, "Help me, God," throughout the day are fine, in and of themselves those things will not cause our relationship with God to deepen. For that, we must spend quality time alone with Him, every day, doing the things we discussed in Rule 2. As you spend time with Him, talk with Him about the barriers that keep you distant from Him, and allow your PM to comfort and lead you. (Rule 5 will cover in depth what to do if you cannot seem to push past barriers like these in your relationship with God.)

Intimacy with God deepens when we have a broken and contrite heart, when our attitude says, "Lord, I mean business. I will do whatever You tell me I need to do. You are more important to me than anything else in my life."

David's life offers a good example of this heart attitude. He longed to feel God's closeness. We see his desire for intimacy with God in many of the psalms he wrote, particularly in Psalm 42:1: *As the deer pants for streams of water, so my soul pants for you, O God.*[NIV] Can you honestly say your soul pants after God? *Selah.*

Later, when the prophet Nathan confronted David about his sin of adultery with Bathsheba, he was full of contrition, as seen in Psalm 51. *Against you, you only, have I sinned.*[v4NIV] David knew that confession was the only way to remove the barrier that was causing him to feel distant from God. He went on to invite God to show him the truth about himself: *Surely you desire truth in the inner parts; you teach me wisdom in the inmost place.... Create in me a pure heart, O God.*[vv6,10NIV]

We will never draw closer to God unless we get serious about our relationship with Him and have a heart attitude similar to David's. Getting serious about God means making Him our primary focus. If the only time we talk to God is when we are on the run or in a crisis, He is not our primary focus. The apostle Paul tells us to *press toward the goal* [Phil 3:14] and to press through distractions and other things that *so easily ensnare us.* [Heb 12:1] When Hezekiah became ill and was told that he was about to die, the Bible tells us he was so desperate to get God's attention that he *turned his face toward the wall* and *wept bitterly.* [2 Kings 20:2-3] God answered his prayer for healing and even lengthened his life by fifteen years. Hannah showed her complete dependence on God when she went before Him *year by year* and *poured out [her] soul before the LORD.* [1 Sam 1:7,15] God answered her prayer for a child, and she grew in her trust in Him, as evidenced by her heartfelt prayer of rejoicing.

If your life seems full of frustration, disappointment, and confusion—sometimes all at once or one right after the other—perhaps it's because you have taken things into your own hands without inviting God's help. If you have left God out of your life, rearrange your schedule so that you can spend some intense time cultivating a deeper relationship with Him. Turn your face toward the wall for a while and shut out the world (or at least quiet it down) in order to focus your attention on Him. Rid your life of extraneous activities, anything that isn't absolutely necessary and that might take your focus off of Him: unproductive conversations, too many secular magazines, sexy music videos, or hanging out with friends all weekend. Spend as much time as you can devoted to learning more about God and sharing with Him the Bad Me and the Very Bad Me. If you do this, your intimacy

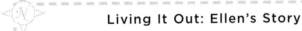

Living It Out: Ellen's Story

Ellen touts herself as a person who "knows a little bit about everything," so she got a reality check when she was talking to a girlfriend about their respective dating relationships. Midway through the conversation, her friend said, "You know, Ellen, you won't be prepared for marriage until you are ready to experience true intimacy. To be honest with you, I think you're afraid of intimacy."

Ellen immediately responded that she was absolutely not afraid of intimacy and that she had already dealt with her fears, thank you very much and praise the Lord.

But after the talk, Ellen realized that her friend might be correct. She decided to talk with God about this and chose to fast and pray, quieting herself down to allow the Holy Spirit to reveal truth. She shut out everything that wasn't essential, including phone calls, television, shopping, and interactions with friends. She even put certain work projects on hold. She dove into Christian books and tapes on intimacy, studied the Word, and reviewed her notes from church and Bible studies. During the process, she wrote down what she believed God was saying to her, mostly in words, but sometimes even in pictures and symbols.

Her PM's gentle but consistent message was clear: "You don't have the corner on the intimacy market that you think you do. You aren't even intimate with Me yet."

At first Ellen wrestled with God about this. She had a personal relationship with Jesus, heard from her PM frequently, and read the Word daily. Didn't all of that equate to intimacy with

God? That's when her PM spoke again: "You think you have let go of certain issues, but you have not. You don't let Me into those spaces; you keep the doors locked. You believe My Word and say you stand on My promises, but that will go only so far if you do not actually believe Me. You are still trying to resolve past hurts, guilt, and shame on your own. You don't trust Me."

As she continued to bring this problem to God, He showed her that her pride was getting in the way of her ability to be intimate with Him and with people. She realized that she was too embarrassed to admit her faults and weaknesses to another person. She was more concerned about other people's errors than her own. Rather than relying on God, Ellen was trying to work out her pain without Him. She was exalting her own coping methods—chatting with friends and getting their opinions—over His healing methods.

When she confessed her sin of pride, God helped her understand that her self-protective behaviors subverted His highest and best purpose for her life in this area—to be able to fearlessly love others intimately, deeply, richly, and unconditionally, especially her future mate. Ellen realized that if she could not let her Creator see into her, she could never achieve real intimacy with anybody else. She came to know that humility and submission were vital keys to intimacy with her future mate.

Ellen made herself vulnerable to God with no other guarantee than that His absolute and steadfast desire was to do her good and to be her Best Friend. Later, she was able to go back to her journals and see what the Lord had taught her through that time. She gave Him her trust—and He has not betrayed it.

with God will grow deeper than you ever dreamed. He promises that you will go from calling Him Master (a revered leader or ruler) to calling Him Husband (a partner).[seeHos2:16]

GET RID OF OTHER LOVERS

When we let God into every part of our lives, He'll point out those things that are destructive to us and our relationship with Him. For example, He may ask you to give sacrificially of your time or money. You may have to say ba-bye to some friends, some goals, some habits, and some hobbies. When we draw closer to Him, God asks us to give up those things that we turn to in place of Him.

These other "lovers" can be anything from gossiping to sexual fantasy to overindulgences with sweets or alcohol or football—anything we run to when we need comfort or love. When we run to these other lovers instead of to God, it stalls the process of deepening our intimacy with Him. We also establish a pattern of self-medicating instead of taking our hurt to the One who can heal us. When we self-medicate, we kid ourselves that we don't need God—or anyone—when we are in pain. This habit not only sabotages our intimacy with God, it also hinders our ability to be intimate with others, including our spouse.

Two married women we know both ended up threatening their otherwise happy marriages by falling in love with romance novels and "lite" music. The mist-covered, lovey-dovey images these other lovers projected and sang about became more and more real to them, and they grew slowly and subtly dissatisfied with their flesh-and-blood husbands. Frolicking "harmlessly" with their other lovers kept them from addressing underlying issues with God and with their spouses. They developed secret lives that they foolishly thought would satisfy. Other lovers never do. That's why we need to cultivate *His* love—the ultimate addiction.

Sometimes the other lovers in our lives may be things that are in and of themselves okay, but when we allow those things to take God's place, they become another lover. For example, several years ago the Lord showed me (Pam) that I had a sports addiction: tennis. Not only was I racking up huge monthly bills at the swank, overpriced club where I played, I was spending time playing tennis that I should have been spending with my family. The Lord admonished me and asked me to take a month off from tennis. (I was going twice a week, sometimes three times, and was a fierce competitor.) In that time He showed me how consuming tennis (and my cute tennis instructor!) had become to me.

Another subtle mistake is to busy ourselves with a lot of activity *for* Him that does not deepen our intimacy with Him. Martha and Mary are great examples of this: Martha started cooking and fussing about when Jesus came by for a visit; Mary sat at His feet, listening. Jesus said that Mary chose the better thing.^{seeLuke10:42} Many people who are active in their church are like Martha. They are so busy attending to the things of God that little foxes sneak into their own garden and spoil the vines.^{seeSongofSol2:15}

Hebrews 12:1 says, *Let us strip off anything that slows us down or holds us back.*^{TLB} What in your life is holding *you* back from greater intimacy with God? What vies with God for first place in your life? Make it your practice to ask Him to search your heart and show you the other lovers in your life. If He brings something to mind, confess it, receive forgiveness, and be sure to repent of (turn your back on) whatever it is and actively refuse to give it the high place it had.

What About You?

Our flesh, which usually wants its way, will rebel as we obey God in this. But if we stay committed, we will triumph. Remember that the proof of love is always measured by the quantity and quality of the time we invest in that love. We don't say we love college basketball and then never watch any games. How much time are you putting into your love relationship with God? Quantity is nothing without quality. Being in the same room with a person isn't enough for the two of you to develop an intimate relationship, even if that person is your spouse. And sitting in a three-hour worship service and singing words out of a hymnal isn't enough to deepen your intimacy with God. Access does not equal intimacy.

Finally, let us enter into this privileged intimacy with God out of love and desire to know Him, not as a work to do in order to find "the one." God already came down and *became* one of us so He could have relationship with us, the creatures into whom He breathed life.seeGen2:7 Then He laid down His life for us and gave us a reason to hope.

How intimate you get with God depends on you. The question is, when He woos you and calls you by name, will you go?

Clean House

If anyone cleanses himself…
he will be a vessel for honor.

—2 TIMOTHY 2:21

Are you the type of person you would want God to send you as a mate? If your gut answer is no, then it's time to clean house! As we discussed in Rule 1, marriage will not solve your problems; it will only expose them. Just like salvation, marriage is a perfect gift, but since we imperfect humans are involved, we must work at it with *fear and trembling.*^Phil2:12 That work begins now! God wants us to enter marriage emotionally and spiritually healthy so that we have something substantial to give to the other person. Dr. Myles Munroe reminds us in his tape series *Male-Female Relationships* that marriage is a "collision of histories." It's true. In order to prepare for marriage, we need to clean out those things in our histories that hinder us from developing the fruit of the Spirit that is essential to any great union: *love, joy, peace, patience, kindness, goodness, faithfulness, gentleness and self-control.*^Gal5:22-23NIV

If you clean out the grimy corners in your life now, you won't bring lingering problems into your marriage, nor will you put unreasonable and ungodly expectations on your spouse. You'll also be in a position to give rather than take in your marriage. You will not need your mate to be a spiritual or emotional crutch for you, but rather you will look to your spouse as your partner.

In this rule we'll talk about how to cleanse our lives of unforgiveness, bitterness, generational sin, sexual sin, and the fallout from past hurts and traumas. (That's a lot of cleanup!) But the good news is that if you have put your trust in Jesus Christ, His death on the cross has already paid the price for your sins and those of your ancestors. Isaiah 53:4-5 says, *He has borne our griefs and carried our sorrows;... He was wounded for our transgressions, He was bruised for our iniquities; the chastisement for our peace was upon Him, and by His stripes we are healed.* We no longer need to be in bondage to these sins, but we must appropriate (take possession of) what Jesus accomplished for us. We do this by confessing and repenting of those sins, and canceling any ungodly ties that bind us to them or to those involved.

As you read this rule, ask your PM to show you the dusty corners in your life. He wants to wipe out even the tiniest bacteria in you. Use the exercises and prayers of confession, repentance, forgiveness, and breaking of ties at the end of the rule so that you may enjoy the benefits of a clean house.

INSPECTING YOUR BEHAVIORAL HISTORY

As you inspect the rooms in your internal house for dirt, be on the lookout for a creeping mold that can prohibit you from having healthy relationships: *unforgiveness.* This sin weighs many of us down and haunts every relationship we try to have. Each time someone hurts us, even slightly, we harbor the hurt. The cycle begins in childhood with our parents (doesn't everything?) and continues to escalate as we encounter friends, coworkers, and romantic partners who "do us wrong." Very often we go into marriage harboring unforgiveness toward those who have hurt us, and also toward God and even ourselves. Sometimes the incidents that triggered the sin of unforgiveness are easy to recall; sometimes they are more subtle. Nonetheless, the Bible clearly commands us to forgive. This is not a suggestion, open to exegetical gymnastics. Jesus said, *Whenever you stand praying, if you have anything against anyone, forgive him, that your Father in heaven may also forgive you your trespasses.*[Mark11:25] And we are all familiar with the Lord's Prayer in which we ask, *Forgive us our debts, as we forgive our debtors.*[Matt6:12] God holds us accountable when we don't forgive.

The message is clear—He is obligated by His Word not to forgive us if we don't forgive others. So if we knowingly hold an offense against someone and refuse to get right with God, we are asking for heartache. We're fooling ourselves if we don't think it will have a negative effect on our marriage. It's a good idea to make it a practice to ask the Lord daily to show you any offenses you may be harboring, known or unknown. After having to apologize to and ask forgiveness of a number of people, you will likely learn to keep your offense list short or nonexistent!

When we ignore God's leading to clean out the spores of unforgiveness, they blossom into a stubborn mold called *bitterness.* This fungus becomes more toxic every time we replay in our mind the injustices done to us (which is what we do when we refuse to forgive). These bitter memories choke out the peace of Christ in our life and compromise our witness. Harboring bitterness is like waking up each morning with a fifty-pound shackle tied to each leg. It wears you out. You may have been carrying it so long that you didn't even notice it was there, but when your PM points it out, you are responsible to address it.

When we harbor bitterness, we often speak harsh, judgmental words toward or about the people who hurt us. Such words are bitterroot judgments. For example, as a child, you may have told your dad, "I hate you! I wish you were dead!" Then as a young adult you may have said, "I'd never marry anyone like my father!" Each time you make such statements, you replay the offense in your mind and the bitterroot judgment sinks more deeply into your heart. Even if you just murmur these things to yourself, you are activating the law of sowing and reaping, harvesting these same bitter judgments on yourself, for God looks upon the heart.^{see1Sam16:7} Scripture tells us that our words carry the power of life and death.^{seeProv18:21}

It's possible to harbor bitterness for so long that we don't even recognize it for what it is. We make our Enemy, the Deceiver, happy when we hang on to secret sins—the ones we convince ourselves didn't happen, aren't there, or won't cause us trouble. But bitterness always leads to the breakdown of any intimate relationship we pursue, slowly but surely. Veteran Christian counselors John and Paula Sandford made a startling observation in their comprehensive book *The Transformation of the Inner Man:* "We have found bitterroot judgments and expectancies in every couple we counsel! [They] are the most common, most basic sins in all marital relationships—perhaps in all of life."⁵ That's why it's critical that you rely on the guidance of your PM. He can help you uncover any root of bitterness that is entrenched in your heart.

It is not enough to stuff down our bitter feelings or to put on a fake smile when we are with the person who has hurt us. God will not be mocked. Let's determine to properly clean out these dangerous molds now, as God points them out to us. Search your heart, and ask your PM to reveal to you people and incidents that were the catalyst for any unforgiveness and resentment you may harbor. He may bring certain people to mind, or He may show you that you have felt bitter toward God. If so, tell Him you are sincerely sorry and ask His forgiveness. A key part of your healing will be to absolve others from any offense you've held against them. The Bible encourages us to confess our sins one to another,[see James 5:16] so we encourage you to speak words of confession and forgiveness in the presence of another believer.

Another area that needs scouring is the dark corner that contains our sexual sins and the ungodly soul and body ties that resulted from those sins. Plain and simple, most of us have piled up garbage in this area, and we need to acknowledge it before God and receive forgiveness. If we simply say, "Everybody does it," or "What's past is past," and leave it at that, we are making a big mistake.

Encouraging Word

*But in a great house there are not only vessels
of gold and silver, but also of wood and clay,
some for honor and some for dishonor.*[2 Tim 2:20]

**If you are the "great house," what "vessels of dishonor"
do you need to clean out?**

To help you better understand the fallout from sexual sin, we'll use a little computer jargon. Every time we become one flesh with a person to whom we are not married, we leave "cookies" behind—traces of ourselves that show where we've been. The Bible uses the word *join* to describe what a man and wife do when they become one flesh.[Gen 2:24] The Hebrew word is *dabaq*, which means "to be joined, to stick, or be

tied together."⁶ This is how God views it when we have sex with anyone. So even though you slipped quietly out of her apartment at 3:00
a.m., part of your soul, spirit, and body was tied to her and hers to you.
You're now connected to her—and everyone else she's ever slept with!
When these ties are formed in a marriage between two equally yoked
individuals, they are godly and good. But when they are formed in a
relationship that violates God's laws, as in incest or fornication (having
sex outside of marriage), they are ungodly and destructive.

Our sexuality is a major target for the Enemy. It is his main tool
in attacking our minds, defiling our reproductive organs, and corrupt-
ing our ability to have healthy, satisfying marital sex. Your brain is the
most powerful sex organ you possess, and he wants it for his own. He
does not want you to marry a godly spouse, enjoy great, godly sex, and
produce other godly "little Christs" in a loving, godly environment.

We need to become "untied" from any other sexual partner we've
had so that we can be properly "tied" to our future spouse.

Inspecting Your Family History

Not only do we need to examine our past behavior, we also need to look
at the patterns of behavior in our family history in order to identify any
sinful tendencies we may have inherited from previous generations. Perhaps a number of people in your family have committed adultery or
succumbed to the bondage of debt. Maybe Granddad had a problem
with lying, gambling, or alcoholism. Perhaps Great-grandma was a
notorious gossip. Sin can be handed down to us by the generations
before us, due to our ancestors' irreverence for God and disregard for
His ways. If you see ungodly traits like this in yourself, it's probably

more than a coincidence! We fuel the fire of these sins when we glibly excuse them, saying, "Oh, that problem just runs in the family!"

As Christians, we are indeed new creatures in Christ. But though our spirit is renewed when we accept Jesus as Lord of our life, our soul (mind, will, emotions) and body may not experience instant renewal. Paul urges us to be transformed by the *renewing* of our mind, implying a continual or ongoing process, not a one-time event.[seeRom12:2] Did all of your challenges and negative behaviors cease the day you became a Christian? Probably not. Deuteronomy warns us that we are to love God and *walk in His ways* in order to receive blessings; otherwise there will be consequences.[see30:16-19] If we don't clean house, we will take those consequences right down the aisle with us into marriage.

INSPECTING PAST HURTS, ABUSE, AND TRAUMAS

The final inspection we need to conduct is on our past hurts. Whether we realize it or not, we all carry around the wounds of past hurts inflicted on us by others, and we need inner healing so that we can love and be loved as God intended. For example, you may have been rejected by a parent, and now you continually reject possible mates before they can get close enough to hurt you. Perhaps a traumatic incident from long ago leaves you frightened, nervous, or unstable in certain situations or environments that remind you of the event. Maybe an uncle, a babysitter, or even a parent violated you sexually as a young child. A study done in 1980 showed that one in every five women in America was sexually molested by a man in her own family.[7] This statistic has only increased with time.

Deliverance from past hurts from abuse and traumatic events

comes as a process, not a quick fix. That means you may need to speak a prayer of forgiveness many times regarding a particular person who has hurt you. Just as you don't recover from internal bleeding overnight, you'll need time for your spiritual and emotional insides to heal from the wound. God understands that you will not always have positive feelings toward someone who has harmed you, even while you are offering a prayer of forgiveness. He is looking for your obedience in confession and repentance, and He promises to take care of the rest. You are only responsible to hold up your end of the bargain. Go through the cleansing steps outlined in the next section, being careful to follow your PM's guidance; He will be faithful.

Be sure that your cleansing process involves *godly* repentance ("I'm truly sorry this behavior displeased You, Lord, and I desire to turn away from it.") rather than worldly sorrow ("I'm sorry I got caught."), as illustrated in 2 Corinthians 7:10: *For godly sorrow produces repentance leading to salvation, not to be regretted; but the sorrow of the world produces death.*

Will you determine to complete this cleansing process no matter what? It will take faith and perseverance, but the rewards will be worth it.

MOLD KILLERS

Here is an overview of the steps involved in scouring your "house."

- *Realize.* Don't deny what your PM shows you about yourself; accept it.
- *Release.* This may involve forgiving relatives, others, yourself, and God.

- *Repent.* Have a change of heart or understanding about the sin.
- *Renounce.* Declare out loud that you reject the sin.
- *Revoke.* Use words to repeal or reverse the power of the sin.
- *Remove.* Apply the blood of Jesus to the sin to cancel it.
- *Replace.* Speak a blessing in place of the sin.
- *Restore.* Ask for and receive God's healing in the specified area.

It is critical that you replace any negative images with the positive ones you acquire as you learn who you are as a believer in Christ. Our "positional truths" form a portrait of who Christ wants us to be. You'll recognize these any time you're reading the Scriptures and you come across verses that include the words *in Him; in, by, or through Christ; in the Beloved; by His blood;* and *in His name.* These truths indicate qualities of Christ that are conferred upon us when we receive Him as Lord of our life.

The apostle Paul exhorts us to stand firm and not allow ourselves to be burdened *again to a yoke of slavery [which you have once put off].*^{Gal5:1AMP} As you clean house, we encourage you to keep a journal of the things your PM shows you and the steps you take to get free. It will serve as a tangible reminder of God's faithfulness to you.

Scrubbing-Bubble Questions

These questions will help you probe into the corners of your past and find the moldy crevices. Answer them honestly and thoughtfully. Note that you are not doing this exercise in order to live in the past.

You are allowing your PM to bring up those things that you may have buried alive so you can look them in the face, repent of any sin, forgive anyone you need to, and be truly set free.

- Are there past boyfriends or girlfriends whose names you can barely speak without disdain? Examine why.
- Are there any past or current behaviors you are ashamed of? Examine why.
- Are there any childhood memories that hurt you to recall? Examine why.
- Are you alienated from a parent or sibling? Examine why.
- Are any chronic physical illnesses prevalent in you or your family? What are they?
- Are any mental strongholds prevalent in your family? (Were you often told things such as, "No man will ever really love a woman" or "All women keep secrets from their mates"?)
- Were your parents true Christians? If not, explore whether there are any spiritual practices in your family line or tradition that would be considered idolatrous according to Deuteronomy 18:10-13.

A GENOGRAM

A genogram is a tool to help identify generational sins. This sample genogram shows how you can complete a genogram of your family.

Once you have studied the example, create your own genogram by copying and filling in the blank genogram to follow. To the best of your ability, write down any distinguishing characteristics about each

GRANDMOTHER/GRANDFATHER		GRANDMOTHER/GRANDFATHER	
Joan	David	Pearl	Malcolm
d. 1979 cancer	d. 1980 suicide	wonderful loving	d. 2001 age 94

FATHER'S SIBLINGS			MOTHER'S SIBLINGS	
Mary	Louis	Joe	Tom	Ann
beautiful achiever	distant divorced	homosexual	estranged from family	d. 1980 mental illness

FATHER	MOTHER
Aaron	Louise
devouted father, quiet	alcoholic

FEMALE SIBLINGS   MALE SIBLINGS

YOU

close relationship — *conflict*   *close relationship* — *favorite*

Judy	Andrea	Darrel	Donald
	major conflict		very close

NOTES:

Louise didn't attend her mom's funeral—angry

family home burned down, 1991

person and your relationship with him or her. Note in particular early deaths, chronic illnesses, infidelities, divorces, incidents of domestic violence, children born out of wedlock, barrenness, incest, poverty, mental instability, ungodly religious practices, and so on.

GRANDMOTHER/GRANDFATHER   GRANDMOTHER/GRANDFATHER

FATHER'S SIBLINGS   MOTHER'S SIBLINGS

FATHER   MOTHER

FEMALE SIBLINGS   MALE SIBLINGS

YOU

This genogram only goes back two generations, but you should go back as far as you can or as far as the Holy Spirit leads you. Note all that He reveals (even if you think it's silly or unimportant). Remember that He leads us into *all truth.* John16:13 You might find it helpful to get your parents' recollections of certain relatives. That's what we did, and we learned things we wanted to know—and a lot of things we didn't!

Prayers of Confession, Repentance, Forgiveness, and Release

Once you have identified the areas that need healing, these simple prayers will guide you through confession, repentance, forgiveness, and release from soul, spirit, and body ties.* The Lordship Prayer is great for Christians as well as for those who want to accept Jesus as Lord and Savior. Start there, and then go through the other prayers as your PM leads you. Be as specific as you can about the things you are confessing. In Mark 10:35, James and John asked Jesus, *Teacher, we want You to do for us whatever we ask.* Jesus replied, *What do you want Me to do for you?*[v36] He wants us to be specific when we pray.

Further ministry and counsel into the areas you uncover may be necessary for complete healing. We encourage you to seek help from a minister trained in healing and deliverance.

Lordship Prayer
This prayer gives God permission to permeate and rule over every room in your house.

> *Lord Jesus, I confess that I have sinned and I acknowledge my need of You. I thank You for dying on the cross for me, and I accept You as my Savior. I invite You now to be Lord of every area of my life—my spirit, my soul, and my body. Thank You, Jesus, that Your blood was shed that I might be set free. Amen.*

---

* Adapted with permission from the Singing Waters Ministries, *Isaiah 61 Ministry School Manual.* For further details, see www.singingwaters.org.

Forgiveness for Generational Sins

Use this prayer for any familial sins that the Holy Spirit has revealed to you. Be as specific as you can.

> *Father, I choose now to confess and renounce the sins and iniquities of my parents and ancestors in the area of _____.*
> *By an act of my will, I now choose to forgive _____ and release them into the freedom of my forgiveness. I release them from judgments and from all debts they might owe me, especially love. I release _____ from all justice I would want to see done. In Jesus's name. Amen.*

Forgiveness for Personal Sins, Including Sexual Sin

Use this prayer for any personal sins for which you need forgiveness.

> *Father, I ask You to forgive me from the sin of _____.*
> *I recognize my own part in choosing to sin in this way and agree with Your verdict on my sin. I repent of this and have a different understanding of how it hurts You when I choose to sin in this way. I now turn from my sin and renounce all pleasure derived from this sin. I ask You to forgive me for all that is past; give me the discernment to recognize temptation when it comes and the strength to resist it. I ask You to set me free from the chains that have bound me to this sin. In Jesus's name. Amen.*

Forgiveness for Bitterness and Related Sins

> *Father, I confess that, as a result of being hurt, I have allowed myself to hold anger, resentment, bitterness, and_____*

*in my heart against _____. I acknowledge this as sin,
and I now repent and turn from this behavior. I ask You to forgive me and cleanse me, in Jesus's name. Amen.*

To Break Soul Ties

*In the name of the Father, the Son, and the Holy Spirit, I break all
ungodly soul, spirit, or body ties that have been established between
myself and _____. I ask You, Lord, to return to me
every part of myself which has been wrongfully tied in bondage to
_____, and I ask that You return to
_____ every part of themselves which has been wrongfully tied in bondage to me, and remove from me all ungodly influence of _____. I ask You, Father, to place the cross of
Jesus and His shed blood between me and _____ and
stop the flow of anything ungodly between us. In Jesus's name.
Amen.*

We'd like to close this rule with this encouraging reminder:

- Jesus came specifically to heal the brokenhearted.[seeIsa61:1]
- Jesus died so you could have life more abundantly.[seeJohn10:10]
- God loves you *in* your sin and desires to get you out.[seeRom5:8]

GET SMART

Now that you've deepened your primary relationship, identified your God-given purpose, and cleaned house—are you ready for love? Not quite. You need to make a few attitude adjustments to prep you for Mr. or Mrs. Right. Before we get together, we need to get rid of our selfish thinking and our worldly ways.

Rule 6 — Put the Kingdom Above the Booty

Rule 7 — Recognize Stop Signs

Rule 8 — Wait, Don't Whine

Rule 9 — Pare Down Your Pals

Rule 10 — Quit Looking Back

Put the Kingdom Above the Booty

The glory of the Lord
will protect you from behind.

—Isaiah 58:8, TLB

Many singles have no clue how to function as a Christian in a dating or courting environment. Too many of us do what everyone else in the secular dating scene is doing. In our quest to find the right person, we go to after-work parties or campus bars, buy clothes we wouldn't show our mothers, live at the hair and nail salon, and position ourselves like heat-seeking missiles at every social gathering, acting like we're enjoying ourselves, all the while crying ourselves to sleep at night.

Some of us have an almost paranoid belief that, *I must be involved with somebody...anybody.* In our overwrought desire to be in a relationship, we experience lust at first sight but tell ourselves it's love. That person becomes the most important thing in our lives, even more important than our relationship with the only One who will ever love us completely and perfectly. We expect him or her to solve our problems, eradicate our loneliness, and be a constant and effervescent cheerleader.

When disillusion sets in, we take directions from our upside-down road map again: *If things don't work out the way I want, I have not found the right person: MOVE ON TO SOMEONE ELSE.* We believe that the next person will be "the one." It's like driving down a highway and following a sign that reads HAPPINESS IS JUST ONE EXIT AWAY, only to exit there and find another sign that says the same thing.

Why do we keep driving down these roads? Because many Christian women don't realize that they are a prize to be cherished while dating—to be unwrapped only after the wedding. And many Christian men don't know that they are to be king, prophet, and priest in their dating relationship and in their marriages. A king is a leader, a prophet gives the vision, and a priest initiates worship. A man should use his leadership, vision, and initiative to keep the relationship pure, healthy, and on track. One of the greatest needs a woman has is security in a relationship. When a godly man actively leads and guides the relationship, a godly woman takes comfort in his leadership (even if he makes mistakes now and again). This is how it should be but often it isn't.

If we hope to attract the Mr. or Mrs. Right who is God's best for us, we will put God's kingdom above chasing the booty—whether that be sex, beauty, money, fame, or fantasy. We will commit to being honest about our relationships and to learning what God says about how to conduct ourselves, and then we will cling to His ways for dear life.

NOTHING BUT THE TRUTH

The trouble is, many of us can't seem to handle the truth. We don't want to follow God's rules. We prefer the relationship lies we tell ourselves: "I don't know why I'm always attracted to ——— [bad girls, emotional infants, rough guys, nitwits, mama's boys, wham-bam Sams…]."

Those of us who admit we have a long history of dating unsuitable people often refuse to search any further for the truth about ourselves and our choices. We prefer denial; it's more comfortable.

The relationship lies that permeate our society, combined with our resistance to truth, make godly living an uphill climb. Even the apostle Paul said, *When I want to do what is right, I inevitably do what is wrong… There is another law at work within me that is at war with my mind.*Rom7:21,23NLT But remember, we don't have to fight this battle on our own. God gave us His Holy Spirit, our PM, to *guide [us] into all truth.*John16:13

I (Pam) had a history of dishonoring God in my dating relationships. Several years ago the Holy Spirit confronted me about this. As I repented and submitted my ways (which were *so* not working!) to Him, He transformed my mind in this area. He gave me His vision for me to be courted with intention, not dated for fun. I learned that His daughters are not supposed to be pinched and squeezed like fruit and then be put back in the bin. He built my self-worth by showing me how very highly He valued me, then He gave me a high charge: to commit to "no kissing" until I was at the altar with my husband. Wow! None of my Christian friends were going that far. But I cherish that charge and fully intend to live it out, by His grace.

This may not be your *rhema,* but God will reveal truth to you. All truth is confrontational; it requires us to make a conscious decision to replace the lies we believe with God's truth. God doesn't grade on a curve. He's designed us for excellence and holiness in relationships and in life, and He would like us not to color outside the lines, please, like we did in kindergarten. We are twenty-, thirty-, and fortysomethings, so let's determine to conquer the sinful nature that Paul spoke about so that we can be free from our old master, sin, in this area once and for all!^seeRom7:14,18

It will not be a cakewalk. The story of the bleeding woman in Mark 5 shows us a picture of what we may face as we seek to honor God in our dating relationships. In the Bible, blood often symbolizes life. For many years this woman's life had been oozing out of her, literally. In her quest for healing, she had been duped by many expensive doctors and charlatans.^vv25-34 Similarly, many of us singles have been duped by quick-fix relationship gurus who sold us their goods on relationships and then flew off to Maui with our $1995 in hand, leaving us feeling empty and defeated. Just as the hostile crowd tried to keep this woman from reaching Jesus, so others will pressure us to abandon or deny God's rules for relationships. Will you press past the voices of the crowd? That's what the bleeding woman resolved to do.

She was fed up with the world's system that had failed her, used her, taken all she had financially and emotionally, and then spit her out and called her unclean. She saw life passing her by, and she was desperate and determined to find hope and healing. She knew if she could just get to the hem of Jesus's coat, everything in her life would change—*had* to change. And did it ever! With fear and trembling, she reached out to Him, and He immediately healed her. When Jesus asked the crowd, *Who touched my clothes?*^v30 she was so overwhelmed that she *fell down before Him and told Him the whole truth.*^v33

There's a pattern for us to follow here: She reached out to Him for healing and told Him the whole truth about her suffering. Many of us need to look in the mirror and admit the truth about why our relationships are not working. Brace yourself as we examine some of the main causes of our relationship disasters.

We Date out of "The Void"

One reason we get involved with unsuitable people in our intimate relationships is that we enter relationships out of The Void inside us instead of The Truth inside us. These unhealthy liaisons seem to make up for the inadequacy we feel in our own emotional tanks and give us a temporary high.

Here are a few examples of what we're talking about:

- A twenty-eight-year-old woman says: "I just like edgy, tough guys like the ones on those music videos. I feel strong when I am around them." *Void: She has not taken the time to find out who she is in Christ, therefore she looks for men who can boost her low self-esteem with their pectorals and their perceived self-confidence.*

- "I like to date the women I meet at work or at clubs," says a thirty-seven-year-old male. "They're cool and more fun to be with. And they're not uptight about sex." *Void: Unwilling to submit to God's command to keep his hands to himself and his zipper up, this man enjoys women who don't require the standard he finds too constricting. He believes he is getting his eye candy and eating it too, but he is sowing a lack of self-control that may ruin him when he's ready for a wife.*

- A thirty-two-year-old woman admits, "I'm attracted to married men. They seem so sophisticated and patient. They really know how to treat a woman." *Void: Too busy or scared to work on herself (and perhaps unresolved issues with her "ex" or her father), so she'd rather go after another woman's man whom she finds attractive but can't really have a committed, godly relationship with.*

- He says: "I don't mind her little hang-ups and neuroses. She
  makes me feel needed." She says: "I can't live without him."
  *Void: This codependent, dysfunctional couple looks cute and cud-
  dly to onlookers, but their relationship only functions because
  both parties are unhealthy. They will become like two ticks on a
  dog's back, sucking the life out of the relationship until it dies or
  until one of them moves on to the next victim.*

Sadly, we convince ourselves that these "Void" partners are safe,
because they feel comfortable to us. Why? Because they facilitate our
sins and dysfunctions. Meanwhile, the precious clock is ticking, and
Satan is ripping apart our soul, dragging us further from God's ideal.
Satan's goal is always to deceive us by any means necessary. He wants
to blind us to the godly mate God desires to bring if we submit to His
rules. Rather than dating out of The Void, we need to allow God to
fill us so that we don't disqualify ourselves from seeing the godly mate
He has for us.

WE THINK WE ARE INCOMPLETE

Another cause of disastrous relationships is that we believe the lie that
fulfillment in life is based on finding the right person rather than on
finding *Him*. But even the "right" earthly mate can only help us
become more like Christ—not more complete. The Word of God says
that we are already complete in Christ.[seeCol2:10] If you don't grasp this,
you will be on an endless search to find someone to "complete" you.

Women, in particular, are often more conditioned to feel incom-
plete if they are not married. This feeling of incompleteness causes
some women to settle for a man rather than wait for God's best. For

older single women, it can evoke a strong desire to have a baby—even without a husband. That's not what your eternal Mate wants for you. It is the result of making an idol of your desires and exalting what the world tells you—"You're getting older, the clock is ticking," "Your parents want a son-in-law and some grandkids," "It's your life, do what you want"—over what He says—"Wait patiently and purposefully for My best. I will not disappoint you."

When God asks us to wait for our earthly mate, we are to do so with an attitude of expectancy, knowing that all things are working together for our good.[seeRom8:28] (See Rule 8 for more on how to wait and not whine.) Take heart from a lesson in the book of Samuel. Israel wanted a king like all the other nations around them. God wanted to be their king, yet He acquiesced and gave them a king named Saul who was tall and good-looking, but He warned the people that it wouldn't be easy. As it turned out, Saul was a psycho. God removed him as king and replaced him with His choice, David, a man after His own heart.[see1Sam8–15] Still, many of us continue to date those good-looking psycho Saul–types that God warned us about!

When you draw from the rivers of Living Water, you won't be enticed to believe the Enemy's lie that you need to have someone's—anyone's—arms around you. Sinking into His arms will rush those thoughts away. I (Pam) learned how to know God this way through a sermon my pastor, Donnie McClurkin, preached. He used the scripture in Isaiah 54, which encourages those who are "barren" to sing and not to fear because our Maker is our Husband. This added a new depth to my relationship with God as I began to see Him as my Mate, not just my Father or my Lord or even my Friend. I learned to hear Him whisper sweet somethings to me at just the right moment and to feel His warm embrace when I needed a hug. He is my Mate until my earthly mate comes to be His tangible representative in my life.

Now for the third helping of truth.

WE SAY THAT BAD IS GOOD

If you hung out with the "in" crowd of teenagers in the eighties you'd know that good was really "baaaad," and cool was really "hot," which was to say, really good. It all got very confusing. Things that were fundamentally good were disdained and things that were essentially bad were admired. When it comes to relationships, do not follow the rules of street vernacular—bad is not good, particularly when it comes to questionable motives and poor judgment in choosing a mate. Samson, who made this mistake big-time, provides an award-winning blueprint of what not to do in this process. Let's take a closer look at his bad (but good) story, which you can find in Judges 13–16.

Here's our modern-day translation of the story: Sam thinks he's ready for a wife. He has not done much internal housecleaning or other preparation for marriage. Instead, he is led by testosterone. He sees a Philistine cutie and thinks she is one hot Jane. Just the way her hips swing and her eyelashes flap makes him crazy with love. He decides he must have her. Sam tells his parents and trusted friends of his decision. They all advise against it and offer sound reasons, but his mind is made up. He decides they just don't understand and insists, *Get her for me, for she pleases me well.*[14:3]

Sam pursues Jane, wins her, and she becomes his wife. Before he can get the girl home from the honeymoon, his downward spiral begins. (Read the rest of the story yourself; we won't spoil the ending.) It was a baaaad scene.

Like Samson, many of us ignore the truth about someone we find attractive. We dig in our heels, fold our arms, and boldly declare that bad is good when it comes to our relationship choices. Despite advice to the contrary, we still insist, "She/he pleases me well." If you find yourself thinking any of the following about people you are going out with, you need a dose of God's truth, or you are headed for a fall:

- *I just know I can fix him/her.* We cannot even fix ourselves, that's why we needed a Savior! So how can we fix other folks, especially when they may resist being fixed? God would not give you an unsaved or unhealthy marriage partner to sap all of your energy and render you useless in the kingdom. If your love interest needs work, it's likely to be work he or she should be doing with the Holy Spirit—alone. Your presence will only hinder the process. Don't date anyone until God fixes the major issues in that person first!

- *I've invested too much time and energy to quit now.* We see the Doppler radar screen flashing: SEVERE TORNADO WARNING: VACATE PREMISES IMMEDIATELY, but we decide to sit tight and see if it will pass. What happens if it doesn't? You may survive—though just barely—to find that your roof is blown off and it will take years to rebuild.

- *I'm scared of what he/she might do if I leave him/her.* You should be more scared of what might happen to your self-esteem, self-respect, and peace of mind if you stay. Your choices are the only ones God holds you responsible for—

only you can choose what's best for yourself.^{seeDeut30:19} Lamentations 1:9 warns, *She did not consider her destiny; therefore her
collapse was awesome.* Do what you should do (break up
nicely), and trust God to do what He does best (comfort and
restore both of you—separately).

- *Well, it's better than being alone.* You think a bad relationship
is worse than no relationship? Wrong. The danger of spending time with the wrong person is that it can cause soul ties
to form: They start out as threads, become wires, and before
long there's a cable tied around your neck, choking you. You
are never alone if you have a relationship with Jesus Christ.
And you have so much to work on to get yourself ready for
the special-sauce mate He has for you, you don't have time to
give in to loneliness!

- *But I luuuv him/her!* Ah, yes. Love can do many things, but
it cannot conquer another person's weak character or usurp
someone's will and force him or her to change. True love
allows the loved one to experience the consequences of his
or her decisions. As my (Chris's) pastor, Dr. A. R. Bernard,
often says, "Suffer the pain of discipline or the pain of
regret."

We Test-Drive the Goods

*It is God's will that you should be sanctified: that you should
avoid sexual immorality; that each of you should learn to
control his own body in a way that is holy and honorable,
not in passionate lust like the heathen, who do not know*

God;… For God did not call us to be impure, but to live a holy life. 1 Thess4:3-5,7NIV

Yet another reason for our relationship disasters is that we engage in sexual compromise. Even though many Christian singles say they don't want to have sex before marriage, we know for a fact they go on overnight trips unsupervised, french kiss, pet, and sleep half-naked in the same bed. And they feel they are honoring God because they aren't "doing it." You are kidding yourself and courting danger. Stop it right now! *Flee sexual immorality.… For you were bought at a price; therefore glorify God in your body and in your spirit, which are God's.* 1Cor6:18,20

Okay, let's be more philosophical: While having sex with someone you aren't married to may satisfy your lust, it is a sad substitute for the intimacy for which your soul longs. Even married couples will tell you that when sex is substituted for intimacy, it is frustrating and empty. If you are going from one warm bed to the next, searching for love, what you need is Jesus. (Sorry if that sounds like a cliché, but it's just true.)

More and more couples who say they are Christians are now living together as a way of "test-driving the goods" to see if they are compatible. No matter what those goofy dating shows tell you, you are not meant to be tried on, worn, and then brought back to the store if you "didn't work out." Couples who live together are playing house. They have an illusion of intimacy but no commitment. They buy homes, open joint bank accounts, and comingle possessions until they have one big stew of mixed property—but no covenant, no wedding ring, no same last name, and no security. Problems arise and things get messy because they have no clear foundation on which to stand. No one knows the rules, so violations are anybody's whim. God has not authored ungodly cohabitation (put his stamp of approval on it), and thus He is not required to finish it (make it work out).[seeHeb12:2] Especially these days, we need His grace to make any relationship thrive.

When we ignore God's teachings in this area, we decide we don't have to commit to one person for the rest of our lives. We get used to "having a back door." This is particularly true for men, who can see such an arrangement—free sex and free meals—as a windfall. But when God brings a mate to a man like this, he'll often experience low-grade guilt and even struggle with feeling trapped in his marriage. *Can a man take fire to his bosom, and his clothes not be burned?*[Prov6:27]

Women are often more vulnerable than men to being hurt when they live with someone they aren't married to. This is because women often agree to the arrangement with the assumption that a ring is just around the corner. When that doesn't happen, even after several years, these women are devastated.

Couples who live together pile up sexual and emotional soul ties daily. False intimacy clouds their decision-making abilities, rendering them unable to make sound judgments when necessary. They sense that the relationship needs to end, but they no longer have the where-withal to think clearly, because they are caught up in the sex and the ensnaring, invisible soul ties. As their judgment becomes impaired, they feel less and less guilty about what they're doing. They know they're doing wrong (especially during the holidays) but push the thought away as the Enemy whispers, *It's fine, everyone's doing it* or some other lie tailored just for them.

Such low-grade guilt strips us of the boldness we need to approach God with confidence.[seeHeb4:15-16] Plus, the Enemy interrupts our attempts at communion with God by bombarding us with the reminder that we deserve whatever we have because we "ain't livin' right!" What a vicious circle.

Engaged couples—you are not exempt! This word is for you too. Engaged is *not* married in God's eyes and neither should it be in yours. Many an engagement has been called off weeks before the wedding. Don't go down this road, especially if you have come this far by faith. Protect yourself by exercising self-control.

Far too many singles lack self-control in their thought lives, which is another major cause of relationship downfalls.

WE LIVE IN FANTASY

When God says we are to live a holy life and avoid sexual immorality, it not only refers to test-driving the goods, it also applies to dabbling in any form of sexual fantasy. *Casting down imaginations, and every high thing that exalteth itself against the knowledge of God, and bringing into captivity every thought to the obedience of Christ.*[2Cor10:5KJV] Men are most susceptible to pornography, women to romantic *imaginations*—both are ungodly activities that we must resist.

Whether it's deceptively called soft or hard, pornography is a deadly problem plaguing our society and our church communities at an alarming rate. With the Internet just a click away, many men in particular are trapped in the web of cybersex. Unlike Grandpa who might have had to sneak a peek at a girlie magazine at the drugstore or bluff his way into the local topless bar, a man or woman today can simply log on in the privacy of their home.

Many single men become habitual porn viewers and have consequently adopted the habit of masturbation. And they think it's just fine. It's not. We've heard this cover-up from Christians: "Well, at least I'm not having sex. I'm not hurting anyone, making any babies, or causing any diseases. What am I supposed to do if I can't have sex?" You may think you're not hurting anyone, but as Fred Stoeker writes in *Every Man's Battle,* which he cowrote with Stephen Arterburn, porn addiction has some pretty nasty fallout. He says that when he was involved with porn, he couldn't look God in the eye, his prayer life was feeble, and his faith was weak. He recalls, "I had no peace."[1]

People who engage in this sin for a prolonged time often create a fictitious composite of the perfect cyberlover, rendering them unable to enjoy a healthy relationship with their real-life spouse. This can be a problem long after a person has stopped looking at pornography. In a book about her husband's involvement in pornography, Laurie Hall reports that researchers have studied what happens in the brain when a person engages in pornography and have found that the brain secretes chemicals that leave behind indelible impressions of the pornographic images viewed.[2] This explains why some people are trying desperately to free themselves from this trap yet can't get rid of the mental images, even though they may have quit viewing pornography long ago.

While men need to exercise self-control about fantasizing with their eyes, women need to exercise control over their emotional fantasies. A man will envision his composite Barbie; a woman will dream about the imaginary Ken doll that meets all of her emotional needs.

A woman who wants to follow His rules also guards against giving her heart away before a man has chosen her to be his wife. She refuses to pursue a man but submits to godly order, allowing a man to labor for her heart, and not vice versa. Michelle McKinney Hammond and Joel Brooks make it plain in *The Unspoken Rules of Love:*

If you get a man through your pursuit, you will never feel
secure because you did the picking.… We can confidently love
Christ because the Bible says that he first loved us. He chose
us and pursued us.… Proof of desire is pursuit. If he's not pursuing you, he doesn't want you.[3]

The woman of God will exercise self-control over her attire as
well, because she knows that what the world says makes her sexy and
attractive is not what God says. She does not lure men to fantasize
about her. She wants no part of catcalls, sexual innuendo, or lustful or
inappropriate comments from male coworkers. Instead, she draws her
self-image from her position as a daughter of the Most High God,
and she walks accordingly. For me (Pam), obeying this meant saying
good-bye to skirts with too-high slits, belly shirts, skimpy bras, and
thongs. What's He telling you?

Self-control for women also means not falling prey to the comparison game—looking at other women with a jealous eye and making snide remarks. Here's a good rule of thumb to put into practice:
Never compare yourself with others in the areas of face (beauty), place
(position in the world), race (ethnicity or cultural background), or
grace (gifting). If you do, you will either develop a superiority complex or an inferiority complex—and neither one is godly.

While the world's paradigm of relationship initially seems appeal-
ing and exciting, we follow it at risk of a great fall. Sharon's all-too-
familiar predicament should sober us: Like King David, great falls can
happen to great people of God. If we aren't careful, we will jeopardize
our self-esteem and even our sanity.

Paul tells it like it is in 1 Corinthians 10:12: *So be careful. If you are thinking, "Oh, I would never behave like that"—let this be a warn-ing to you. For you too may fall into sin.*[TLB]

WE FALL HARD AND SUFFER LOSS

Aptly titled, a book in the Old Testament called Lamentations illus-trates what happens when we ignore His ways. Jeremiah, the author of Lamentations, is called "the weeping prophet" because of his deep

Living It Out: Sharon's Story

In my late twenties I began to wonder if the phrase *real Christian man* was an oxymoron. So I began to accept dates from a man who went to church, even if he didn't "walk the walk." Although I considered myself a mature Christian, I let my desire for companionship influence me. I knew in my heart that it was wrong for us to have sex, but I gave in to my desires anyway. Sometimes I gave in simply because I felt this was what I needed to do in order to "keep my man." Satan would whisper, "Sex is only natural. A relationship can't grow without it" and then the clincher—"If you don't, someone else will." I always felt guilty after sex, but I made excuses. Like Adam and Eve, I found myself hiding from God because I felt I had disap-pointed Him.

When I found out I was pregnant, I experienced the truth of the scripture that says that all darkness will be brought to light. I realized too late that God's rule about compassion for the Israelites. Here, he is, uh…lamenting…about the sad state of Judah and Jerusalem, knowing their destruction is around the corner: *Her uncleanness is in her skirts; she did not consider her destiny; therefore her collapse was awesome; she had no comforter. "O LORD, behold my affliction, for the enemy is exalted!"*[1:9]

Jesus offers the same message in parable form in the book of Matthew: *But everyone who hears these sayings of Mine, and does not do them, will be like a foolish man who built his house on the sand: and the*

sex outside of marriage was in place to protect me from suffering and pain. (Although "safe sex" would have protected me from pregnancy, it wouldn't have protected my spirit from brokenness and shame.) I realized that my "church attender" and I had very different beliefs, so in addition to having "everyone know my business," I would now have to face the challenge of becoming a single mother. I was excited about having a child but upset that I had grieved the Holy Spirit. I no longer wanted to publicly profess that I was a Christian because I was ashamed and afraid of being called a hypocrite (although I still prayed and read my Bible fervently).

I learned an important lesson from this: I cannot depend upon someone else to be moral for me or to be responsible for my actions. I have to prize my body and view it as a precious gift to be treasured, otherwise no one else will. So now I delight myself in my God and in my daughter. I tried my way and failed, so now I'm doing it God's way.

rain descended, the floods came, and the winds blew and beat on that house; and it fell. And great was its fall.[7:26-27.]

Both passages teach us that if we operate in the flesh and don't consider our future, we are headed for an awesome collapse. Paul takes this a step further and tells us that when we fall we lose something we may not get back: *For no other foundation can anyone lay than that which is laid, which is Jesus Christ…. If anyone's work which he has built on it endures, he will receive a reward. If anyone's work is burned, he will suffer loss; but he himself will be saved, yet so as through fire.*[1Cor3:11,14-15]

Encouraging Word

Are you in a relationship with a nonbeliever
or someone who is lukewarm in his or her faith?
If so, stop now and ask your PM,
"How will _____ and I walk together
toward marriage unless we agree?"[seeAmos3:3]

While this passage is discussing the rewards of the afterlife for Christians, it has implications for singles in good-looking relationships that are built with tissue paper and Elmer's glue. They do not endure. You do not want to "just get married," with your clothes smelling like smoke! You may rejoice that you've found "the one." You may sport a Tiffany engagement ring and plan the biggest ocean-side wedding your town has ever seen, but you will suffer loss because your relationship is not based on God's Word, nor was the decision to marry guided by the Holy Spirit.

The loss you will suffer in such a marriage will be characterized by

- a feeling of emptiness, even when you're together;
- an eerie and pervasive feeling that you made a mistake;
- a sense of estrangement from your spouse, even while you sleep in the same bed;
- a deep sadness when you realize your spouse doesn't share your faith-based values or beliefs.

Will you agree to rest in God's arms until He brings the man or woman He has for you? Will you allow your spirit—instead of your mind or your body—to lead your decision making? This next section breaks down the how-tos.

Spirit Reigns: Soul and Body Follow

When we are committed to operating out of our spirit—the part of us that has been renewed by God—rather than out of our soul and body, we can put the kingdom above the booty. Let's explore what it means to let our spirit reign.

The apostle Paul teaches that we are tripart beings. He says, *Now may the God of peace Himself sanctify you completely; and may your whole spirit, soul, and body be preserved blameless at the coming of our Lord Jesus Christ.* [1 Thess 5:23] Note the order in which Paul talks about our makeup. He says *spirit, soul, and body,* not body, soul, and spirit. You might expect that he would mention the body first, since that's what we see and spend our time feeding, clothing, and primping. However, this is the world's view of a person's makeup—outer things rule. On the contrary, when God creates something, He always starts with the inside, the spiritual or the spirit, and then works His way to the outside.

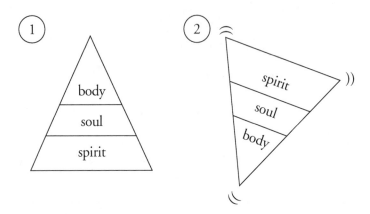

The two diagrams above illustrate how God sees us versus how the world sees us:

Our *spirit* is the part of us that communicates with God. Our spirit was awakened from sleep when we surrendered our life to Jesus. *God is Spirit, and those who worship Him must worship in spirit and truth.*[John4:24] If your spirit isn't alive, you cannot worship Him. (If you're not sure if yours is alive yet, turn to page 69 and live!) Our soul is that part of us that communicates with us—our mind, will, and emotions. Our body is that part of us that communicates with our environment.

Each of our three parts is wed to a certain outcome in our lives. For example:

- Through our *spirit* God is constantly saying, "Live holy," "Live by My Word," "Raise your standard," "Follow My example," "Don't compromise and the outcome will be great."
- Our *soul* is bent on pursuing our earthly desires unless our spirit intervenes. "C'mon, you're getting older. Just date and/or marry him; he's fiiiine," "She loves me and I love her.

What difference does it make if she doesn't know the Lord yet? It'll work out."

- Our *body* deals with our physical cravings, which almost always conflict with the value system of the spirit. The Bible refers to our body as "the flesh." It will say things like: "Everybody needs sex; God will understand if you sleep with him just this once" or "You're not having sex; it's just mutual masturbation. No one's getting hurt." The outcome here can be deadly.

Everything we do—including the way we date someone—needs to be guided by our spirit rather than by our soul or body. This order will make a huge difference in how your life—and your desire for a godly mate—turns out!

Are you currently in a relationship that's based on the booty rather than on the kingdom? If so, run! We're sorry, but you simply cannot follow both the world's way and the Word's way, so choose today which one you will serve. Here are some steps you can take to keep unsuitable characters away from your heart:

- Frequently examine your motives for seeking or being in the relationship. Make sure they line up with the Word of God and are not based on any of the voids we illustrated earlier.

- Take some time alone to put your current relationships through your PM's magnifying glass. If the person you are dating doesn't reflect God's character and is not building His character in you, resolve to let that person go. Go back and follow the steps in Rule 5 if you need help. Ask God to give you the strength to move away from relationships that are dragging you down or disturbing your peace. This is a key step. You can learn more about how to break up in Rule 14, "Handle the Heat." Our prayers are with you to make this crucial step toward your destiny.

- Ask God to bring the right person into your life. Listen carefully to Him as He tells you where to go and where not to go, what to join or commit to, and what to leave alone.
- Be ruthless in repeating these steps until they are habitual.

WALK LIKE A MATURE SON

God has established parameters to help us have fabulous marriages. We ought to embrace them the same way we would hug a security guard who yelled "Duck!" because he saw a bullet coming at our heads.

Romans 8:14 says, *For as many as are led by the Spirit of God, these are sons of God.* The Bible uses two different Greek words for "son." *Teknon* is someone who is a son by mere fact of birth. *Huios* means a mature son.[4] The son this verse is talking about is *huios*. As you choose to put the kingdom above the booty, you are deciding to leave the Teknon clan to be part of the Huios family. Welcome!

Now you can daydream about how wonderful it will be to have that beautiful, godly mate who will pray with you, make love with you, raise children with you, advance the kingdom with you, and laugh with you as you look forward to the days to come, having no fear of old age.[see Prov 31:25] Rain will come, but you will have confidence in those storm windows you installed when you were single and followed His rules.

Recognize Stop Signs

They tried to go…
but the Spirit did not permit them.

—Acts 16:7

Tara and Len were inseparable. They attended events together all over their town. After six months, Tara began to ask Len how he felt about her. Rather than answer her question, he'd tell her, "I think about you all the time." Tara was thirty-six, and her emotional and biological clocks were ticking loudly. So she increased her efforts to get Len to begin talking marriage. She cooked for him, changed her makeup, and began wearing more sexy clothing. He complimented her on her new look and her great chicken dishes, but every time Tara probed about how Len felt about her, she got the same response, "Can we talk about this later, babe?" No matter what she did or said, Len continued to brush her off whenever she brought up the subject of marriage.

One day she called Len at work to demand a status report. He was preparing for a big presentation and said he couldn't talk but would call her back. Two hours later he still hadn't called. Frantic, Tara kept hitting the speed-dial button on her phone every ten minutes until she got something other than his voice mail. When he finally answered, he was incensed. "Don't you understand English?" he asked her. "I said I would call you later!" Len did call later, apologetic. He explained that he just couldn't be pushed into marriage until he was ready. He asked her to bear with him while he "worked things out with God."

Do you see the stop signs in this true story? If not, you will by the time you've finished reading this rule! God gives us stop signs when He knows we're going to get hurt in a relationship. Our PM waves a red flag of warning, alerting us to danger. When we are in a relationship, we must keep our eyes open for these stop signs and obey them when they appear. If we miss them, like Len and Tara did, we'll end up staying in the relationship a lot longer than is good for us, or worse, we'll marry someone who is not God's best for us.

When we are blinded by love (or what we believe is love), it is harder to discern fatal flaws in the other person. They are near perfect in our eyes. Compatible with us in every way. A match made in heaven.

Not.

If you want to ensure that you won't ignore the stop signs, we encourage you to be a person of integrity. Be sure that you understand what it looks like to have God's peace in a relationship.

ARE YOU INCORRUPTIBLE?

A person of integrity is incorruptible, "incapable of being bribed or morally corrupted." Is that you? First Peter tells us that when we were born again we were implanted *not of corruptible seed but incorruptible.*[1:23] Our spirit is the only part of our being that is insulated from the corruption of the world. When we have integrity, our outer lives and our inner lives are in alignment; our behavior matches our morals, our values, and our words—particularly in our dating relationships. If you are expending all your energy leading a double-dutch life, you'll be too distracted to see the stop signs.

One of our most valuable assets is our reputation with others, but the highest form of integrity is having a good reputation with ourselves. This requires frequent self-examinations to ensure that our behavior is above reproach. It requires that when something goes wrong in our lives, we accept personal responsibility rather than blaming others or shaking a fist at God. Integrity acts as an invisible force field around us that protects us from self-sabotaging behaviors, such as becoming involved with people we shouldn't.

Here are some guidelines for becoming a person of integrity:

- Resolve never to lie under any circumstances or to participate in a lie.[seeEph4:15,25]
- Decide what is right before looking at what is possible.[seePs119:11]
- Commit to doing what is right, even if it is not popular or if it differs from what you've done in similar situations in the past.[seeIsa43:19]
- Treat everyone the same way, regardless of how an individual treats you.[see1Pet2:18-23]
- Resolve to accept complete responsibility for your behavior and expectations.[seeDeut30:19]
- Be sure that your conduct is so exemplary that you can tell others that they should follow your example.[see1Cor11:1]

Does this list intimidate you? Don't let it. While it may not be easy to develop a strong character, it is a sure way to help you get into a right relationship. As you commit to develop Christlike integrity in yourself, you will stop being attracted to those people who don't have

the same high standards you have. You will no longer move forward
in a relationship if your PM tells you, "Stop."

Do You Know What Peace Is?

You will greatly enhance your ability to recognize relationship stop
signs if you understand what God's peace is when it comes to romantic relationships. Unfortunately, we have experienced so much misery,
dysfunction, and weirdness in our dating relationships that we mis-
takenly believe these things are normal—even when our PM is telling
us, "Get out now!" Many of us think dating equals drama and drama
equals stress, and that's just the way it is. But the pain of broken
promises, sexual compromise, pressure, deceit, hardness of heart, verbal abuse, and constant miscommunication is not the norm for sons
and daughters of the Most High King in relationship with other sons
and daughters of the Most High King! Don't allow your past mistakes
to cause you to confuse problems with peace. Webster says *peace* is "a
state of tranquility or quiet; freedom from disquieting or oppressive
thoughts or emotion; harmony in personal relations." *Strong's Concordance* (everyone should have one) says it means "prosperity, well-
being, wholeness, a safety that can bring feelings of satisfaction." We
can only have this sense of intactness and safety when our relationships are in line with the Word of God.

The problem with this for many of us is that we get caught up in
a counterfeit peace because we're in luuuuv. Here's an example: Tootie
is drawn to Mookie because he's "such a good person." He volunteers
at a homeless shelter twice a week and has a great heart. The only
problem is that whenever she brings up her faith, he says that's good
for her but he doesn't need "all that." Tootie, continuing to date him

and watch his good works, is beginning to talk herself into the idea that the relationship is an equal yoke. She says, "Mookie does more good things than 90 percent of the Christians I know. He never curses. He's so generous and has a great relationship with his family. I think it's okay." (Wink, wink.) The problem is, her Relationship Counselor, the Holy Spirit, never winks.

Faith and an active relationship with God must drive the engine powering your relationship. Feelings are only allowed to be the caboose. If these two things are out of order, you will not have peace and your train will derail.

Remember, the Bible is your manual for how to become and attract Mr. or Mrs. Right and have a successful relationship. Your PM is the 800 number you should contact for tech support. He will never tell you something that doesn't line up with the Word of God. So it's likely that Tootie is not reading God's Word—or else her PM would lead her to stumble upon 2 Corinthians 6:14, which clearly says, *Don't be teamed with those who do not love the Lord.* [TLB] Whatever version of the Scriptures you choose, that verse will never say, *team up with a 'good' person.* [TOOTIE]

We have talked with many men and women who want to grow in the things of God, yet are being held back by Nominal Charlie (who works every Sunday or likes to sleep in) or Jezebel Julie (who doesn't understand why you both can't lounge around her apartment in your undies on the weekends and then go to church). The degenerative impact of dating people like this is more subtle and can be confusing because they profess to be bona fide Christians. Their outward demeanor is couched in some form of spirituality that may really be a counterfeit bill.

Paul warned that in the last days there would be people *having a form of godliness but denying its power.*[2Tim3:5] He went on to say: *Stay clear of these people.*[MSG] As Christians we are not to conduct our relationships like the world does. God says we are not to be yoked with an unbelieving or lukewarm person.[see2Cor6:14]

And another thing: If you think you can go out with not-yet-believers and convert them while you date, you are deluding yourself and being dishonest with the God you say you serve. It is a lazy road and its best end is mediocrity.

Here's an example of what can happen when we handle a relationship dilemma like this God's way. Maria was dating Chaz, who was a great guy but not a believer. The dating was getting serious, so Maria told her sisters, also Christians, about Chaz. They met him and all agreed he was indeed a great guy—but she shouldn't date him because he wasn't a believer. She continued to date Chaz for a time but was in constant angst. Her sisters counseled her to end the relationship and honor God above her feelings. Maria cried her eyes out, but followed their advice and the leading of her PM. She channeled her pain into service at her church's Sunday school. Meanwhile, she and her sisters prayed, fasted, and cried out to God that Chaz would come to know Him and that the relationship would be renewed. Three months after she stopped going out with him, Chaz accepted Christ. A month after that, Maria and Chaz got back together. He began attending church with Maria regularly and showed a strong appetite for the things of God. A year later they were married. Today, they have four lovely children, and Chaz is a leader in their church.

Maria let go of her "catch" because she knew that if Jesus isn't in the fishing boat, it will sink. She followed after peace, not feelings. The Bible talks about peace 429 times! Jesus said, *Peace I leave with you, my peace I give unto you: not as the world giveth, give I unto you. Let not your heart be troubled, neither let it be afraid.*[John 14:27 KJV] Paul reiterated this in the book of Philippians, *Do not be anxious about anything, but in everything, by prayer and petition, with thanksgiving, present your requests to God. And the peace of God, which transcends all understanding, will guard your hearts and your minds in Christ Jesus.*[4:6-7 NIV]

These scriptures suggest that peace...

- is given to us by God;
- does not come from our own reasoning or understanding;
- is something internal that will guard our heart and mind from being troubled, anxious, or afraid even when circumstances say we should be.

We need peace if we are going to make it to lifelong love!

Women may have an easier time following after peace because they are naturally intuitive and more in touch with their feelings. For example, a wife will say to her husband, "I can't put my finger on it, but something doesn't seem right about him." The husband may be clueless to the feelings behind what she's expressing, but if he's a wise man of God, he'll pay attention to his wife's lack of peace. Men can sometimes be drawn by greed, ambition, or lust that camouflages their lack of peace.

On the flip side, women who allow their feelings to rule are likely to stay in troubled relationships out of a need to feel loved—by anyone. An insecure man who constantly needs a woman to affirm his masculinity will also have murky judgment about peace. Proverbs 19:2 says, *It is not good to have zeal without knowledge, nor to be hasty and miss the way.*[NIV] So men and women have something to learn from one another when it comes to staying grounded and holding on to peace. It's a wonderful thing when single men and women have godly, platonic friendships with each other and can gain valuable perspectives from "the other side." (See Rule 12 for more on this.) But our final answer about what peace is must come from the Word.

Remember, if you are telling your friends, "God told me so" about someone, know this: The unrevealed will of God (what you believe you heard from above) must always submit to the revealed will of God (what's already been proven in the Word of God). That means you do not have the right to exalt what you "heard" above what the Bible has to say. Put what you heard to the Hebrews 4:12 test and allow the Word to cut *swift and deep into our innermost thoughts and desires with all their parts, exposing us for what we really are.*[TLB] The passage goes on to say, *He knows about everyone everywhere.*[v13] That means He knows about the person you are dating or courting (or hope to date or court)—and He's happy to tell you what He knows![see Jer 33:3]

Here's an exercise to help you identify the areas in your life that disturb your peace, especially those that are relationship related: Draw a line down the center of a page. On the left side list all the areas in your life that cause you stress or rob you of peace. On the right side list specific actions you can take immediately that would bring these stressful areas of your life in line with your inner values and convictions. If there are clear actions you can take to address them, great. If not, take it to your PM and get greater clarity on how to move the mountain—especially if it's a "him" or a "her."

GET OUT OF UNSAFE RELATIONSHIPS

People of integrity who follow after peace value themselves and their inner sanctum more highly than anyone or anything else. They also hold the people they are dating to the same high standards. That

means they stay away from anyone who exhibits any of these dangerous characteristics or behaviors:

- poor people skills (rude, brusque, overbearing)
- makes excuses or blames others rather than taking personal
  responsibility for problems
- complains and surrounds themselves with other complainers
- expects failure
- is stubborn and unwilling to learn from others
- has an undisciplined lifestyle, prone to irrational, impetuous
  decisions
- tends to be crushed by failure

I (Chris) believe that complaining is the most toxic of these behaviors. Think about how much time we waste complaining to others
about our lives, particularly our relationships with the opposite sex.
Whether it's happening in the locker room or on the cell phone, complaining is a dangerous and unrewarding energy drain. Complaining
replaces objectivity with frustration, adding emotion and stress to an
already unhappy situation. Complaining creates an inaccurate, negative picture of life that is out of line with biblical truth. Furthermore,
it's contagious: Complainers attract complainees. If you don't recognize the complainer as a stop sign, this person will wear you out.

Not only do we need to recognize the toxic behaviors that are
relationship stop signs, we also need to be able to recognize toxic relationship patterns—both in ourselves and in those we date. Over the
years, the two of us have observed several types of daters who can hem
others into ugly, painful, unsafe relationships. If one type doesn't
apply to you or your situation, another might, or it may apply to a
friend. We've named them: the Waiter ("We've been dating about

eight years…we're just waiting for the right time to get married."), the Evangelist ("Oh I just *know* he's going to get right with God any day now."), Mr. and Mrs. Po Tential ("So what if she smokes a little weed on the weekends. She has a good heart."), and the Siren ("He's the hottest guy I've ever dated. I can't let him go!").

The Waiter

Len, Tara's boyfriend, whom you read about at the beginning of this chapter, is a Waiter. This type of dater is the seemingly stable Christian who clearly demonstrates a growing relationship with God. You are inseparable and hop from church event to church event attached at the hip. You have been dating for so many years, he or she is practically part of your family. But when the question of marriage comes up, this boyfriend or girlfriend changes the subject.

Analysis: Check to see what the root of the delay is. You may unearth fears about losing freedom or being a parent, or you learn that this person is trying to hide something from you. How long you date or court a person depends on how mature the two of you are and whether your preparation is complete. Make a *qualitative* assessment to determine this rather than a *quantitative* one. One friend began dating her now-husband at the tender age of sixteen. Both sets of parents insisted they finish college, so they waited to marry at twenty-one. But at thirty-six, you don't want to date someone for five years—that's why we urge you to get dieseled and get smart before you get together!

The Evangelist

An Evangelist dater is the man or woman who is drawn to someone, usually because of appearance, and seeks to either convert that person to Christianity or "help him or her grow" as a Christian. The person is often an immature believer who is excited to be dating someone he or she can "be themselves" with, without any pressure to live up to standards of sexual purity or other biblical principles.

Analysis: The Word is clear; we are to stay away from *unequal yokes.*^{see2Cor6:14} God understands the consequences and collateral damage these kinds of relationships cause His sons and daughters. You can have all the reasons in the world why you must have this unbelieving boyfriend or girlfriend, but God says none of them are valid.

Mr. and Mrs. Po Tential

Mr. and Mrs. Po Tential profess a relationship with Christ. They follow all of the rituals, speak "Christianese," and know all the tunes in the hymnal, but their hearts are far from God. They are just as apt to spend a night out partying as they are to be at an all-night prayer meeting. The nominal Christian is drawn to them because they represent the path of least resistance. Seasoned Christians can be reeled in by them if they take their eyes off Jesus and focus on their loins or their biological clocks.

Analysis: People with potential are only one notch above the unbelievers that the Evangelist dater gets involved with. Technically, you are following the letter of the law if you are dating this kind of person, but 2 Corinthians 3:6 says *the letter kills, but the Spirit gives life.* Yes, he or she is a professed Christian, but the spirit of the law asks: Does this person share your resolve to live according to God's ways? You don't have to look far to find "technical Christians." Neither do you have to search for sad stories of people who married them. Would you want a husband or wife who's "technically" faithful to you? Did you want to be "technically" forgiven by God for your sins when you prayed to receive Christ? No, you want to experience these things, not just see them on paper.

Casualness in this crucial area will result in casualty.

The Siren

These men and women are drop-dead, show-stopping gorgeous. Every head turns when Sirens walk into the room. The person with them is secretly and openly envied by most of their friends and acquaintances, and enjoys it. They make you look *so* cool.

Analysis: Too many of us secretly desire a trophy wife or husband. But 1 Peter 3:4 warns us that inner beats outer: *Let it be the hidden person of the heart, with the incorruptible beauty of a gentle and quiet spirit, which is very precious in the sight of God.* It's a rare Siren who has as much wisdom as they do comeliness. Many are like King Saul— tall and good-looking, but unstable in emotions and character. The people who "ooh!" and "aah!" over your Siren spouse at every dinner party will not fill the void that will grow in your soul year after year if you married a mannequin.

OBEY FIRST, ASK QUESTIONS LATER

The stop signs in the situations we presented are relatively easy to discern. But sometimes God just tells us no about someone, and at the time we can't see why. We need to obey first and ask questions later, knowing that He always operates in our best interest—He's our Father. Often, hindsight will prove twenty-twenty. When He says no, He is saying, "I have something better." Our awesome God always sees our lives from the blimp and gives us regular traffic reports when we need them, so we can drive safely on the highway below.

Wait, Don't Whine

Do not fret—it only causes harm.

—Psalm 37:8

I f you've read the story of Abraham, Moses, or Joseph, you've come face to face with people who had to wait years before they received a gift that God had promised them. All of them had to persevere and learn some things before they received the promised blessing. Abraham waited decades for the son God had promised.[seeGen17:3-6] Moses, a prince and a scholar, spent forty years tending sheep in a foreign desert before God used him to deliver the Israelites from slavery in Egypt.[seeExod14] And young Joseph (Remember him? He's the dream-coat guy whose story is told in Genesis 39–50) dreamed about his future greatness more than a decade before he saw it realized.[seeGen37]

Sorry, things have not changed. Waiting is still an essential part of God's sovereign plan. Some of us will wait longer than others for a mate or to see a calling fulfilled, but a whiny attitude makes the wait even longer! Even worse, it's counterproductive. *How* you wait makes all the difference.

Many singles squander valuable time because they don't have the right perspective on The Wait. They grow sour and sarcastic because they believe they have "waited on God" for a mate and are still wait-ing after many years. We're not talking about feeling lonely on certain days of the month or during the holidays—everyone goes through that, even many married folks. We're speaking to singles whose attitude is, "I'm fed up and ready to throw in the towel."

We say, go ahead—throw it in. But do it with the right attitude: If you've completed your part, meaning you've made all the changes and adjustments your PM has alerted you to, then you can relax, have peace, and let Him do the God part. Throw *God* the towel, and cast all your concerns about finding a mate on Him, because He cares for you.see 1 Pet 5:7

Encouraging Word

Your attitude should be the same
*as that of Christ Jesus.*Phil 2:5 NIV

It makes a huge difference whether the nose of an aircraft is pointed up or down when it is flying. If your attitude toward relationships were the directional gauge on a plane, would you be positioned to soar or to crash? What can you do right now to avoid a catastrophe?

But few of us can throw the towel to God because we still need it to clean ourselves up! As we pointed out in Rule 3, waiting on God is not a passive activity. The Hebrew word for "wait" is *qavah,* which means "to look for, to hope, and to expect."[5] Even the scholars who wrote Webster's dictionary define the term in a positive light: "to stay in place in expectation of, to remain stationary in readiness or expectation, to look forward expectantly."

There is much to do while you wait. Scripture says, *Delight yourself also in the LORD, and He shall give you the desires of your heart.*Ps 37:4

The Living Bible says it more aptly: *Be delighted with the Lord.* This simply means: Enjoy life with Him. Don't focus on what you don't have yet, delight yourself in what you have now, and wait in joyful anticipation of what He's going to do next. Of course, this takes effort, and God knows this. That's why He also says, *Do not fret.*[Ps37:8]

We can do this if we believe that God...

- is a good God who created marriage,[seeJames1:17]
- commanded us to be fruitful and multiply,[seeGen1:22]
- is no respecter of persons,[seeActs10:34]
- hears our fervent prayers,[seeJames5:16]
- cares about our desires,[seePs37:4]
- knows us intimately,[seePs139:13-16]
- is sympathetic to our frailties,[seeHeb4:15]
- is longing to be gracious to us,[seeIsa30:18]
- is delighted to give us the kingdom,[seeLuke12:32]

We should have joy while we wait for Him to bring our mate!

BENEFITS OF WAITING

Let's face it. Many of us didn't get our act together spiritually until we were adults, even though we may have known about God and the Bible or made a verbal commitment to Christ at a young age. This puts the majority of us in a position where we must now redeem the time we lost during our evil days.[seeEph5:15-16] To redeem means "to buy back or make amends for." While we are ladies- and gentlemen-in-waiting, we need to use every opportunity to develop the fruit of the Spirit in our lives.

If we keep our relationship road map right-side up and follow the

What's in Your Fruit Box?

Take a moment and examine your own fruit and the fruit of
the person you are considering dating. Is it tasty or spoiled?

Fruit	Question
love	Does this person love sacrificially? seek to love others?
joy	Does this person have an exuberant spirit, a joyful heart? Is he or she stable in bad circumstances?
peace	Does he or she exhibit the peace of Christ? a calming nature?
patience	Is this person disciplined enough to delay gratification? (This is a big one!)
kindness	Does he or she show kindness? Is he or she devoid of cruelty and "mean streaks"?
goodness	Does this individual have strong morals and stand up for what is right?
faithfulness	Is this person consistent, honest, and faithful?
gentleness	Is he or she truly sensitive to your needs?
self-control	Does the person control his or her mouth, spending, habits, and sex drive? Does he or she cause you to live a more morally pure life or a less morally pure life?

guidance of our PM, we can reap some tremendous benefits during this season of singleness. Remember, God is waiting for us to become a person who is ready to receive the mate He has for us. It's really not that deep. For instance, He may know that you will cause less stress for your spouse if you learn to be on time, lose weight, and pay off debts, or He may want you to curb your tendency toward sarcasm or angry outbursts because of how it would hurt your mate if you don't. One of the reasons He has us wait is to develop us and prepare us so we can have a marriage that glorifies God, right? Right. Then don't waste time whining—you've got work to do!

The benefits of biblical waiting are outlined in Isaiah 40:31: *But those who wait on the LORD shall renew their strength; they shall mount up with wings like eagles, they shall run and not be weary, they shall walk and not faint.* Note the four active phrases in this verse. We have expounded on each of them here:

We Gain Strength

[They] shall renew their strength.

Sometimes we feel weak and even intimidated when we pray for something and don't see immediate results. But when we seek God out, study His Word, cultivate our relationship with Him, and honor and worship Him while we wait, He takes our weakness and gives us His strength. Just as Clark Kent of Superman fame ran into a phone booth when he was in a jam, so we can run to God's throne for "a change" when we are weary. When we accept Jesus as our personal Lord and Savior, an exchange takes place—our sins for His abundant life. (If you desire this exchange, turn to page 69—we'll meet you by the phone booth.) When we go to Him with our brokenness, loneliness, and sadness, He exchanges them for strength and gives us the power to wait with joy. As we do this again and again, the schism between what we are promised as children of God and our current reality lessens.

Some additional verses follow that express this promise:

- *For the eyes of the LORD run to and fro throughout the whole earth, to show Himself strong on behalf of those whose heart is loyal to Him.*^{2Chron16:9}
- *He gives power to the weak, and to those who have no might He increases strength.*^{Isa40:29}
- *You have turned for me my mourning into dancing; you have put off my sackcloth and clothed me with gladness.*^{Ps30:11}

We Get a Bird's-Eye View

They shall mount up with wings like eagles.

When we rely on our PM for guidance and direction as we wait for our mate, He raises us up like an eagle flying over the earth, enabling us to see the big picture and adjusting our perspective. We begin to appreciate that we have time to ourselves, freedom of movement and choice that we wouldn't have if we were married. We can see areas in our life that are still immature, selfish, or unfinished, and we can also see how those flaws would be compounded if we were married. This motivates us to draw up a plan for how we can get ready for marriage, and when we see what we need to do, we realize that we have much to focus on while we wait.

We Store Up Extra Energy

They shall run and not be weary.

Some of us run for exercise and know that it can be hard to keep going, especially when it's an uphill grind. Professional runners eat special carbohydrate bars and down fancy electrolyte drinks in hopes of storing up energy to finish the course. As we aim to wait biblically on our mates, we too are running to win. As Paul says plainly, *So I run straight to the goal with purpose in every step. I fight to win. I'm not just shadowboxing or playing around.*[1Cor9:26TLB] So we eat the Word of God, drink in His presence, and store up extra energy, just as Popeye did when he ate his spinach.

What do we do with all this extra strength? We use it to accomplish the things the Holy Spirit, our PM, has been leading us to do. We work on our plan, clean house, and transform our mind with the Word and other great books, tapes, and CDs; we hang up on booty calls, go to Bible studies and teaching seminars, share our faith, serve the body of Christ, have good, clean fun, and we stop whining. Stored energy also helps us handle inevitable difficulties with new strength and a conquering spirit.

We Walk Worthy

They shall walk and not faint.

As the Lord whispers reassurance to us on a daily basis, we feel increasingly more invincible and develop a determination to persevere. The

Bible is very clear that our faith will be tested, but He puts steel in our bones to prevent us from cracking!

Many of us wilt when our faith is tested too much or for too long a period. We look to ungodly or unhealthy ways of easing the tension when we're under pressure. But this is when we must deepen our resolve, knowing that we may feel weak *because* we are almost at the finish line. A psalm that reflects back on Joseph's life says that between the time God spoke to him about his great future and the time that promise came to pass, *the word of the LORD tested him.*[Ps105:19] Popular leadership author John Maxwell notes, "An older English translation of that passage states that *iron came into his soul.* Adversity shows a person his mettle."[6]

The Enemy may try one more time to tempt us to abandon God's ways and to take things into our own hands. He wants to test *whose* we are. That's when we must grit our teeth and show him that our bones are made of steel!

THE LONG AND WHINY ROAD

Many singles look good on the outside but are whining on the inside. We are smiling deacons, ushers, and children's church workers, but our inner dialogue is worried, fearful, and sarcastic. If you've been walking as a Christian for a while, you've probably seen that we can have great faith and boldness in one area of our lives and none in other areas. We can boldly declare the promises of God for our financial provision, our health, and our unsaved loved ones, yet be unsure about whether He'll bring us a wonderful mate.

If this is you, take comfort. David felt the same way. Psalm 42:5

records him talking to himself, saying, *Why are you cast down, O my soul?... Hope in God.* (This is a great illustration of what we mean when we say the soul is where *you* communicate with *you*.) Six verses later, he was still troubled, so he told himself again to hope in God.[see42:11] In the next psalm, he encouraged himself a third time, saying the same things.[seePs43:5]

We will always have an internal tug-of-war between faith and fear. After all, Satan wants to turn us into spiritual schizophrenics. Like David, we need to be proactive about telling our will and our emotions, "Remember, you are trusting in the Lord. So do what the Word says, and don't be anxious about finding a mate. Quiet down and get in line." Do this as many times as it takes for you to stop going down Whiny Road.

When we whine we are saying, "God, Your way is too hard and, by the way, it's unattainable. I'm sorry, but I'm just going to do it my way." We elevate our opinion above God's. That's called idolatry. Giving in to whining also lowers our resistance and weakens our resolve to stay sexually pure. When our resolve is weakened, how will we have the energy to speak to our will and emotions to keep them in line? Jesus said, *For out of the abundance of the heart his mouth speaks.*[Luke6:45] We can only speak what's in our heart. If it's full of doubts and complaints, that's what we'll express to ourselves and to others.

But that's not the only negative fallout of whining rather than waiting on God. Let's examine what else will happen if we fail to develop our character and become the person God wants us to be.

Galatians 5 provides a compelling comparison between who we become when we choose to wait productively, led by the Spirit, and who we become when we don't. *The Message* captures the meaning of this scripture in all its living color:

> *Why don't you choose to be led by the Spirit and so escape the erratic compulsions of a law-dominated existence?*
>
> *It is obvious what kind of life develops out of trying to get your own way all the time: repetitive, loveless, cheap sex; a stinking accumulation of mental and emotional garbage; frenzied and joyless grabs for happiness; trinket gods; magic-show religion; paranoid loneliness; cutthroat competition; all-consuming-yet-never-satisfied wants; a brutal temper; an impotence to love or be loved; divided homes and divided lives; small-minded and lopsided pursuits; the vicious habit of depersonalizing everyone into a rival; uncontrolled and uncontrollable addictions; ugly parodies of community. I could go on.* Gal5:18-21MSG

Wow! That list is not pretty. You may not fall into all or even most of these traps, but even a few can be lethal to your goal of becoming and attracting a godly mate. Let's look at each one more closely:

- *Repetitive, loveless, cheap sex.* You can fall prey to the lie that you must be in someone's arms to feel good about yourself. You look to complete yourself through fly-by-night relationships because you fail to recognize that you are already complete in Christ.
- *A stinking accumulation of mental and emotional garbage.* Your self-esteem will suffer as a consequence of your having engaged in shallow relationships. If you struggle with this, make this your new computer screen saver: ANYTIME I

COMPROMISE MY STANDARDS OR MY MORAL PURITY I LOWER
MY PROPERTY VALUE.

- *Frenzied and joyless grabs for happiness.* In an effort to medicate your loneliness with over-the-counter solutions, you rest-
lessly run from one thing to the next, trying to drown your
sorrows. Your grabs for happiness may lead you to run up
your credit cards, eat too much, or find yourself belly up at
a bar or zonked out in a stranger's bed. As you drive down
this road of ever-elusive fulfillment, you will continue to see
road signs that tell you happiness is just one exit away. So
you keep driving until you run out of gas.

- *Trinket gods; magic-show religion.* You will follow those who
tell you, "Hey, *you* are god." You will capitulate to the advice
on the latest radio talk show and chat about it with your
coworkers at lunch. You will follow prescriptions from *Cos-
mopolitan* or *Maxim* and other sensationalist magazines that
flood your supermarket checkout counters. You will slowly
drift away from the value system of Christ and begin embrac-
ing the world's way.

- *Paranoid loneliness.* Your singleness will be the object of all of
your waking thoughts and nighttime dreams. Proverbs 23:7
says, *As he thinks in his heart, so is he.* All your focus will be on
how alone you are. When you are tired of whining to yourself
about your status, you will call a friend and whine some more.

- *Cut-throat competition.* You will view social settings as if they
are game shows in which you must attract the most attention from the opposite sex by the time the evening ends.
You will view every other member of your sex as a roadblock

Living It Out: Priscilla's Story

My name is Priscilla, and I am a reformed whiner. My heart's desire since high school was to find a godly husband, get married, and have children. I was in a relationship for five long years, but it ended painfully in a broken engagement. Many other relationships began with promise but ended up going nowhere. When I turned thirty and was still single, the real whining began. Going home for Christmas was a bittersweet experience because all my siblings were married and had kids. I felt confused and hurt that I was the only one who didn't have a family of my own.

I was starting to become bitter, though I tried to hide it. My prayers often went something like this: *Lord, what are You doing? I've been a good girl all these years, not only going to church regularly but also teaching Sunday school. I've kept myself sexually pure, and yet my colleagues at work who hop in and out of bed with their boyfriends end up getting married and seem to be doing just fine! I'm missing out!*

One day when I had stopped whining for a moment, He told me: "You are indeed missing out—on an abundant, joyful, fulfilling life I want to give you right now." That's when it struck me. I had been saved since I was ten, but because I had been so focused on my desire to be married, I had no peace. I thought that by being obedient, I was somehow entitled to get what I wanted, when I wanted it. Then when things didn't turn out as I had hoped, I felt entitled to whine, and I even began to question my Christian faith and seriously doubt God's goodness.

For the first time in years, I got my eyes off myself and began to see all the needy people around me. I served in my church with reckless abandon. I found great fulfillment in helping others, and even though I dated no one for years, I was the happiest I had ever been—really. When my husband, Steve, and I did meet, I was so content with the Lord and with my life that I didn't want a relationship! But God brought me around, and a few months after I turned thirty-six, we were married. The day I accepted Steve's proposal, I threw myself on my sofa and wept for a long, long time. God's grace overwhelmed me. After years of shaking my fist in His face and whining, "Why, why, why?" I understood that He had been patiently keeping me, tenderly waiting for me to find in Him the source of my hope, joy, and expectations.

These words from Psalm 62 are etched in my memory: *I stand silently before the Lord, waiting for him to rescue me. For salvation comes from him alone. Yes, he alone is my Rock, my rescuer, defense and fortress. Why then should I be tense with fear when troubles come?*v1-2TLB to your desire. Inst ead of looking to represent God's king-dom in your social settings, you will promote and build *your* kingdom.

- *All-consuming-yet-never-satisfied wants.* This can be best explained as the When-Then syndrome. "When I get this, then I will be happy," "When I make seven figures/sing a solo in my megachurch/have a child/appear on *Oprah*/drive a Beemer/move to the burbs/move to the city/get my doctor-ate/have an extreme makeover/run for public office/fill in the blank, *then* I'll be satisfied." Not so.

- *A brutal temper.* Do you find yourself getting angry with God because your friends are married and you're not? This is a sign of a bitter whiner in the making. If you continue down this path and refuse to wait on the Lord, you will find your-self becoming a cranky, bitter, cynical person no one wants to be with.

- *An impotence to love or be loved.* Bet this caught your atten-tion! Impotence, as we know thanks to the Viagra frenzy, is an inability to...rise to an occasion. You become so self-focused that you never develop the ability to love someone else (which requires you to be other-focused) or to receive love in a healthy way. Any marriage you enter in this state will eventually die. Another good screen saver: LOVE SEEKS TO BENEFIT ANOTHER AT THE EXPENSE OF SELF, WHILE LUST SEEKS TO BENEFIT SELF AT THE EXPENSE OF ANOTHER.

- *Divided homes and divided lives.* You are constantly compro-mising your convictions, trying to reshuffle the deck, hoping for an ace. Your sensitivity to sin can become nonexistent.

(This must be how people have two and three families at a time in the same city!)

- *Small-minded and lopsided pursuits.* You may start doing crazy things, such as emptying out your savings to get a sky box at the Super Bowl just to impress someone or quitting your job to become a model when you're five foot two and bowlegged.
- *The vicious habit of depersonalizing everyone into a rival.* You are forever sizing everyone up and so miss out on developing good friendships.
- *Uncontrolled and uncontrollable addictions.* You may spend many fruitless nights trying things that bring no permanent solution to the pain.
- *Ugly parodies of community.* Misery loves company. Satan can dupe us into thinking we have sympathetic ears in the bartender, the gossip, or the married man. These are poor imitations of the fellowship and support Christians can have with other Spirit-led believers.
- *I could go on.* Paul could have pointed out even more ugly consequences of not choosing to cultivate the fruit of the Spirit, but maybe his inkwell was running dry!

WHAT GOD WANTS

God wants us to become fully mature. Always remember that. He waits for us to be who we need to be to receive the blessing of a mate and to be ready for the challenges of marriage. He desires to see the fruit of His Spirit in us, but that requires our cooperation. Although we may not even be aware of it, and though we may not like it one bit, God wants to use our time of singleness to prepare us. If we are willing, He will be diligent about helping us reach our *teleios*,[7] or our "finished, completed end," that we may *come...to a perfect man, to the measure of the stature of the fullness of Christ.*[Eph4:13]

Finally, the prophet Isaiah said that four good things will occur when we trust God and wait on His timing: We gain new strength, get a better perspective, store up extra energy, and deepen our determination to persevere.[seeIsa40:31] As we allow God to change us, the mustard seed of faith in our heart will become a focused fire.

Decide today who you will be: a waiter or a whiner?

Pare Down Your Pals

In the multitude of counselors there is safety.

—PROVERBS 11:14

When you determine to do things God's way—especially in your relationships with the opposite sex—some of your current friends and supporters may balk, even those who say they love God and have a relationship with Christ. We tend to expect, optimistically, that everyone in the faith is trying to grow in the things of God. They're not. Some of your friends may distance themselves from you because you have little interest in the same old gossip and no longer want to do things that compromise your faith walk. Anticipate this loss, and understand it when it hits.

Better yet, do the paring yourself. Only people whose lives encourage you to grow in your relationship with God qualify to speak into your life—particularly when it comes to your love life. God will be faithful to bring you new friends as you obey your PM in this area.

Letting go of old cronies is no easy task. Some of them you've known since high school or college or your first job. You've partied together, barhopped together, played together, laughed, cried, and dished the dirt together until your phone batteries died or until there were no more good Blockbuster videos left to rent. But now that

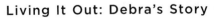

Living It Out: Debra's Story

Most of us see friendship as eternal. After all, a friend loves at all times, right? But as I grew in my faith, I grew more distant from some of my friends. Two in particular come to mind.

Celina and I had been friends for ten years, but then she and her husband went through a divorce. She would call me frequently wanting to talk, and it often seemed like we were on different pages. Sometimes I just could not pick up the phone to call her back—for months. I used to apologize for that (or even lie and say I had lost her number), until I realized that I just didn't want to call her. While part of me wanted to be there for her, God revealed to me that I had a messiah complex. I was an enabler who was also trying to be Celina's savior. God showed me that continuing a close friendship with Celina would be destructive for both of us. After some prayer, I realized that it's not my assignment to "be there" for everyone. I felt peace about allowing Celina to become an acquaintance rather than a close friend.

I also had to cut close ties with another good friend I've had since high school. It was fun talking with Charlotte, but our conversations always seemed to revert to the same tired jokes and stories from our teenage years. When Charlotte told me she was having an affair with a married man, I began to speak a hard line into her life, showing understanding but being firm about the fact that she had to end the affair. Charlotte saw a different, more mature Debra, and she couldn't handle it. She still wanted us to be teenagers trying to find ourselves and dishing the dirt. I no longer needed or wanted these conversations.

At first I was at a loss about what to do because I kept thinking I needed to be her friend. But she didn't want godly counsel; she wanted to tell me about her affair as a form of entertainment. I finally had to say, "I'm really sorry, Charlotte, but I can't continue this friendship." And I listed all the reasons. She was upset and angry—and rightly so. I had never set up any proper boundaries in our friendship during all those years. She had no warning for the bomb I dropped. It was an awkward conversation, but our friendship has found its rightful place as a result.

I was entering a new season with God, and Celina and Charlotte represented the old season. If a friendship is going to survive these kinds of changes, the old patterns in that relationship must die and be corrected as we mature in our faith—and my friendships with Celina and Charlotte couldn't make the change. Since this paring down, the Lord has brought godly women into my life with whom I can be myself; women I can pray for one day and then turn around and ask for prayer the next; women who encourage me rather than drain me. My close friendships now are mutually empowering. The iron in each of us gets sharper as we enjoy one another and benefit from the awesome gifts each one brings.

you've gotten serious about God, you go to His throne for counsel more often than you go to the phone. You don't think their jokes are quite as cute, and you find yourself having less and less interest in their conversation in general. They either don't want to hear your God-centered gab or will give you a polite, "Uh-huh," and carry on with their nonsense.

It's time to pare down your pals.

DON'T LISTEN TO UNGODLY COUNSELORS

When you are trying to make major changes in your conduct and align yourself with God's standards, you can no longer walk after evil counsel, as King Ahaziah did in the Old Testament, to his undoing.[seeChron22:3] Ahaziah's dad, Jehoram, was king of Judah before him, and the Bible notes that when he died, it was *to no one's regret.*[2Chron21:20NIV] (That's pretty sad.) Jehoram was also a descendent of King Ahab, described as more wicked than any other king of Israel.[see1Kings16:30] Instead of taking note of his disastrous heritage and attempting to turn the country back toward God, Ahaziah listened to the advice of his mother and his father's evil counselors, which led him to ruin. Don't make the same mistake. If your friends aren't encouraging you to follow God's ways, don't allow them to continue to speak into your life.

Old friends can be like a favorite pair of old tennis shoes or like Mom's peach cobbler. The shoes have holes and the pie is making us obese, but we still like them—maybe even feel we *need* them. In His mercy, God may do to us what He did to Gideon. When Gideon was getting smug in his own power, God stripped down his army from thirty-two thousand to three hundred men, just to keep him honest and remind him of who's in charge.^{seeJudg7:2-7} Ungodly cronies can keep us from facing a truth that God wants us to see. He may remove them from our lives to draw us back to Him as our primary Counselor.

So prayerfully decide who should be your close friends, your "just friends," and your acquaintances. This list may shift several times as you grow in Christ. When your *Friend* ship gets filled with people of noble character, remember that their counsel is not only for fair weather. Be willing to listen to their hearts even when you don't agree with or want their advice.

Don't Ignore Godly Counsel

Most of us gravitate toward people who will give us the opinion we want to hear: that friend who will be thrilled to learn of our new, attractive girlfriend and will indulge our sexual innuendoes regarding her; or that friend who will tell us that moral compromise is par for the course if we want to get married before the century's over. Even worse, when we do get godly counsel, we often ignore it. That's what Jehoshaphat and Ahab did.

The story is told in 1 Kings 22. (Get ready for more strange, tongue-twisting names you can hardly pronounce.) Jehoshaphat, the king of Judah, and Ahab, king of Israel, wanted advice about whether to attack the king of Aram and retake Ramoth Gilead. Initially they asked the advice of four hundred false prophets, and all of them said that if Israel and Judah attacked, they would be victorious. Then they asked Micaiah, a prophet of the Lord, and he told them *not* to attack because, if they did, it would be a disaster.^{see1Kings22:23}

Ahab didn't like Micaiah because he never prophesied anything good—meaning he never told Ahab what he wanted to hear. Ahab preferred the false prophets who did. So even though Ahab had insisted that Micaiah tell the truth, Ahab rejected it and put him in prison. Guess what happened? Jehoshaphat and Ahab led their armies to fight the king of Aram—and it was a blow out. Ahab was killed. This story illustrates the truth of what Jesus said in Matthew 7:14: *Small is the gate and narrow the road that leads to life, and only a few find it.*^{NIV}

False prophets are alive and well and living in your town! They don't care about what God wants, they simply tell us what we want to hear. Humor us for a moment. What do you really want from the people you go to for advice? Let's say you are Jehoshaphat and you aren't sure about the character of the potential Mrs. Jehoshaphat you are dating. You are concerned and worried about a number of issues regarding her, but you really like her and don't trust your ability to be objective. You ask all the "guyz and gurlz" for advice, and they say, "Go forth!" However, there is that one godly friend whose opinion you haven't asked, and your PM keeps prompting you to do so. When you do, that person is the lone voice saying, "Don't do it!"

What would you do?

Our prayer is that you won't seek validation for what you want, but that you will only seek counsel from your PM and godly counselors.

Let Big Brother Watch

If you are in a relationship, you need to do more than simply seek advice from those you know listen to God. We recommend that you find a few godly friends who can serve as your accountability and prayer partners as you court your potential Mr. or Mrs. Right.

This means your relationship needs to be in the open. If you are engaging in backseat lust, you probably won't follow this advice because you don't want to expose yourself to scrutiny and disapproval. But if you are following His rules for relationships, you'll want to ensure that things remain righteous. You will welcome godly input and counsel so your purposes are not disappointed and your plans won't fail.^{seeProv15:22KJV}

Encouraging Word

A word spoken in due season, how good it is!^{Prov15:23}

**Has someone you know ever pointed out
some flaws in your relationship with your boyfriend
or girlfriend? How did you react?**

So how do you choose an accountability partner, and what exactly does that person do? First of all, you need a pool of godly friends from which to choose. Candidates should exhibit the fruit of the Spirit—love, joy, peace, long-suffering, kindness, goodness, faithfulness, gentleness, and self-control. Their lives don't need to be perfect, but they should be people you admire and respect. Specifically, their own dating relationships or marriages should be godly. Your accountability partners must also be trustworthy, as you are going to share your heart with them. Make sure you allow time to test the character of any person you consider asking to fill this role in your life.

If there isn't a peer that fits the bill, don't discount people older than you. We can learn from both their victories and their errors, especially if they have been faithful, committed Christians for a long time. For example, Ruth had a great counselor in her mother-in-law, Naomi. She schooled her in the protocol of how to approach Boaz, according to the custom of the land, to be her kinsman-redeemer. In the New Testament, Paul was a mentor to Timothy. He gave this young pastor valuable counsel on how to conduct himself in the churches Paul had established.

Accountability partners provide your relationship with safety because you have given them the authority to ask pertinent questions about your conduct, intentions, struggles, and most of all, about what you are hearing from your PM. We've both benefited from having a godly friend hold us accountable, formally and informally. Here's our recommendation for how to spend your time together:

- Meet weekly, and try to meet for less than an hour.
- Ask each other questions that pertain to the weaknesses you have previously shared. For example: How is your thought life? prayer life? financial life? What is God teaching you about yourself? What are you learning about Him?
- Spend some time praying for one another.

This last year I (Chris) have enjoyed an accountability relationship with a male friend. We meet weekly for thirty minutes of prayer and support of each other regarding our relationships, moral purity, integrity, and character. We talk about specific situations and value each other's input. This gives me, as a man in full-time ministry, the opportunity to share what is on my heart that week. It's an important outlet to have someone trustworthy who will listen to me without judgment. I talk about my dating relationship, and he talks about his relationship with his wife. He points out areas where he thinks I should be more flexible (which are many). I encourage him on how to be king, prophet, and priest in his home. It's been invaluable to have an older married man speak into my life as a single man. We close our time with a prayer for increased mental purity—every man's battle.

See a Relationship Doctor

If everything about the person you are considering marrying has checked out—you have peace in your spirit; you have tested his or her character; you've seen evidence that this person is growing spiritually and has the same values you have; and you have sought the counsel of godly friends who have given you thumbs-up—it's a great time to see a Christian counselor together or attend a premarital weekend conference.

If we wait to get counseling until after we've become engaged, sent out the invitations, chosen a china pattern, and put money down for a catering hall, few of us will turn back—even if it becomes painfully clear in a premarital class that we should reconsider. Sometimes we need the help of a professional, godly "outsider" who can help us determine whether to move ahead to engagement. Secular counseling is not an option here, for obvious reasons. Unless counselors can look at your relationship from a biblical perspective, they can't guide you in God's ways.

It's disturbing to note the lack of substance in premarital classes given by some churches. Many of these classes are done "by the book," without much one-on-one feedback by a pastor or church leader who will challenge couples on tough issues. Marriage counseling should never be a simple formality. Just ask the now-divorced couples who swore they were madly in love and could make a marriage work. Are you really exempt? Don't kid yourself. See a doctor instead.

You can go to a Christian counselor or conference together when you are serious but not yet engaged. (Stay in separate hotels!) Do this in addition to the premarital counseling your pastor may require in order to marry you. When it comes to marriage, take all the godly counsel you can get! Read books, devour tapes, go to church seminars—your PM will show you what to eat and what to spit out.

How do you find a good Christian counselor? We recommend that you get a referral about the counselor's competence and manner from another person or couple you know. Everyone who's licensed isn't a great counselor, so don't just flip through the yellow pages under *C*. Keep in mind that most men will only go to a counselor they can respect, one who exhibits strength of character, and most women want a counselor they can relate to, one who has a good bedside manner. Take each other's needs and preferences into consideration, and make sure you're both comfortable with your choice, especially if you are going to multiple sessions (which we recommend).

Here are some questions you can ask to help evaluate a Christian counselor on the first visit. Does this person…

- speak the truth in love?
- respectfully confront? (There *should* be a degree of discomfort every time you leave his or her office.)
- point out things you haven't seen in yourself before?
- get you and your Mr. or Mrs. Right to broach subjects that neither of you have been able to talk about openly before?
- offer you more Bible-based counsel and solutions than personal testimony? (Biblical principles out of Matthew and

Mark are always better than examples from "me and Mable.")

- seem to have a heartfelt desire to help you have an excellent relationship?

If the two of you decide to part company based on the advice of your PM and your accountability partner or counselor, don't lament too long. God has just saved you from a lifetime of pain and regret! (For more on breakups, read Rule 14.)

Your Boaz or Rebecca is on the horizon, if you'll still believe.

Quit Looking Back

Do not remember the former things.

—ISAIAH 43:18

Have you noticed that the front windshield of your car is much larger than the rearview mirror? This is partly because automobile designers feel we should spend more time looking in front of us than we do behind us. God feels the same way. He wants us to look forward to the great destiny He has planned for us. He doesn't want us to stay focused on past failures or even past successes.

Mistakes are part of everyone's autobiography. Even if your background is "pretty clean," the Word says that *a righteous man may fall seven times.*^Prov24:16 Some falls are hard, and the *ouch!* is easy to recall, while others may be more subtle. We need to identify them, move past them, and get ready to rise again. The same is true for the good things in our past, our "glory days." We can't keep reliving them either.

Many of us crucify ourselves emotionally as we hang between the two criminals called If Only and What If? They sound something like this:

If only…

- I had married that person I dated five years ago.
- I lived in a city with more single men (or women).

- I hadn't been so reluctant to propose.
- I hadn't worked so hard for so long to advance my career.

What if...

- I hadn't left that great job? I could almost retire by now!
- I don't ever have any children of my own?
- I hadn't gotten hurt as a college athlete? I'd be on ESPN today.
- I don't get asked out on another date?

These criminals are punishing singles all over the world! It's important for us to learn from our past so we make better choices, but we need to keep moving forward into the future God has planned for us. Let's take a look at two areas where we get stuck in the past: the Land of Regret and the Island of Glory.

LEAVING THE LAND OF REGRET

Far too many of us live in the Land of Regret, listening to the accusations that the Enemy whispers in our ears about past mistakes and failures. He wants us to feel that it's too late to turn things around.

Here are some of the areas Satan uses to try to discourage and defeat us:

- *Wasted time in a dysfunctional relationship.* Many of us have regrets about wasting months, even years, in relationships that we knew were unhealthy. We never felt any real peace about the other person, yet we couldn't seem to break the emotional ties that had been formed. And if we compromised ourselves sexually in the relationship, the soul ties created made the bond even harder to dissolve. Finally, one of you called it quits, leaving the other feeling regretful and discouraged. Satan will do his best to keep you beating yourself up for not getting out of a bad relationship sooner.

- *Sexual failure.* If you commit a sexual sin after coming to Christ, you'll feel more guilt than you would if your moral failure occurred before you were a Christian. As a Christian, you know that God prohibits sex outside of marriage, and so you knowingly disobeyed Him. Few things will steal our joy as quickly as living a double life as a Christian. As one person said, it's like being in the Civil War and wearing a shirt from the North and pants from the South. You end up getting shot from both sides! The Enemy chimes in with, "How could you have done that? And you call yourself a Christian? Are you really saved? God's not going to forgive you of *that*."

Encouraging Word
Your PM may be saying to you, Do not remember the former things, nor consider the things of old. Behold, I will do a new thing.[Isa43:18] *If so, what's keeping you from going where He's going?*

- *Divorce.* If you have been divorced, you acquired shackles of shame and guilt that are hard to shake. You carry the burden of breaking one of God's commandments (which many of us do daily in other areas). The spiritual and emotional toll of divorce weighs heavily. You likely experienced a painful change in friendships, living environment, family dynamics, and financial stability, as well as an upsetting change of identity.

You may have a sense of weirdness in your church environment if people have sent you nonverbal signs of disapproval. The Enemy will badger you constantly with, "Who are you? You're secondhand goods." And the inevitable: "What are you going to do now?"

- *Financial mismanagement.* People usually make this mistake only when they begin to make money and can take out loans and run up credit card debt. If you have acquired unmanageable debt due to impulse shopping or overspending, the Enemy will mock you, saying, "Look how old you are, and you don't have a thing to show for it." Then he will taunt, "Who would want to marry an irresponsible person like you?"

- *Lost time.* We can lose time in many ways: pursuing money or a career rather than God and His destiny for us; or wasting time in a dead-end job simply because we are too lazy or unmotivated to seek God's best for us. We may consider the years before coming to Christ as lost time, or we may have lost time due to an addiction of some kind.

As I (Chris) worked on Wall Street for ten years, I ran across many people who were caught up in climbing the corporate ladder, only to get to the top and realize that it was propped against the wrong wall. Many of the women executives I knew seemed to be hit harder by this because they woke up in their forties and suddenly realized they wanted a family after all. Their biological clock (read: the Enemy) was yelling, "What are you going to do? You can't hug your 401(k) at night. It can't give you a child. You wasted all your time."

QUIT LOOKING BACK141

Do you have regrets? Once you have identified them, submit them to God. He redeems the time for us. He promises to give us a double portion for our former shame[see Isa 61:7] and to restore to us all that the locusts, caterpillars, and canker worms took from us.[see Joel 2:25] He always gives us the opportunity to grow stronger, wiser, and healthier. All it takes is cooperating with our Personal Mentor as He does His mighty cleansing work. *Therefore we do not lose heart. Even though our outward man is perishing, yet the inward man is being renewed day by day.*[2 Cor 4:16]

GETTING OFF THE ISLAND OF GLORY

Others of us get stuck on the thrill of looking back at "the good ol' days." You can recognize people who are stuck on this fantasy island a mile away. With wistful looks on their faces, they are always bringing up stories about how things used to be. (No, not the sweet way your grandfather does it.) They can stay up until 2:00 a.m., recalling how that old boyfriend used to send flowers every single week, or how much they liked the perfume that a former girlfriend always wore ("What was it again…?"). Nothing wrong with talking about old times, but we say if it goes on for more than twenty minutes and there's a catch in your voice while you talk, you are making love to the past.

You may be stuck on these old glories:

- *A past relationship.* You thought it was so good—until your heart was crushed. Your love interest told you he or she wanted to move forward—without you. You have moved on physically, but not mentally or emotionally. Now you have more faith in how things were in that relationship than you do in future possibilities. Or perhaps your relationship was dysfunctional and God liberated you from it, but now you look back on those days and think a little slice of something bad is better than 100 percent of nothing.

- *Public recognition you once received.* The roar of the crowd still sounds in your ear at night as you recall memories of public accolade. Perhaps you were a budding sports celebrity, a hot musician, a top salesperson, or a young genius. God saw fit for that season of fame to end, yet you are still stuck in the memories the cheers, the awards, the perks, and the love. The Enemy wants to dupe you into thinking that God is done blessing you, when in reality He's only just begun. But you can't, or won't, get out of His way so that He can accomplish this new thing in your life.

A story in the book of Ezra further illustrates the problem with living on the Island of Glory. It tells of a group of people busily preparing to build a new temple for the Lord. This new temple would replace the famous one built by Solomon years before. All of the best logs were cut for wood, skilled masons and carpenters were called in—everything was ready. The young men appointed to oversee the work were psyched. Everyone praised the Lord with trumpets and singing—everyone except the old men, that is.

> But many of the priests and Levites and heads of the fathers' houses, old men who had seen the first temple, wept with a loud voice when the foundation of this temple was laid before their eyes. Yet many shouted aloud for joy, so that the people could not discern the noise of the shout of joy from the noise of the weeping of the people.[3:12-13]

What a huge contrast in emotions! While the younger men are celebrating, the older men are weeping because for them nothing could compare to the splendor of the temple Solomon had built. The same issue caused one group to burst into song and another to break into tears. The older men, wed to what God had done before, could not embrace the new thing He was about to do.

Many singles are unable to celebrate today because they are stuck in yesterday's glory. If a night of light-hearted reminiscing with old friends turns into tears on your pillow when you get home, we're talking to you. If you are wed to the past, you will spend all your energy trying to recapture or lament something that will never be the same again.

Lots to Leave Behind

God wants you to leave the Land of Regret and the Island of Glory so He can take you into something better. If you don't go, you may never be ready to receive the destiny God has planned for you, including your future mate. The story of Lot's wife in the book of Genesis illustrates how we can perish in the Land of Regret. Interestingly, the Bible only refers to her as Lot's wife. God told Lot to get out of the city of Sodom because it was an evil place, and He was going to destroy it. Lot's wife was in conflict over the move. Simply put, she was stuck in one place, and God was trying to take her to another; she couldn't let go of the old digs to embrace the new. God gave them clear instructions not to look back at the city as they were leaving. But Lot's wife couldn't resist—she had to take one last look, and as a result of her disobedience, she got salted.[seeGen19:26]

When you get attached to your environment or lifestyle, it's hard to extricate yourself from it. It took forty years to get Egypt out of the

Israelites. They were so accustomed to being slaves that they couldn't adjust to freedom. God was constantly saying, "Don't do this" and "Be sure to do this," and they constantly rebelled. It seemed that although they were being shown a great future, they were too afraid to walk forward. When are we going to learn that when God says no it means no, and when He says go it means go? When we try put a

Living It Out: Roxanne's Story

My divorce ended an almost twelve-year marriage. I went through more than just a change in tax status, residence, and lifestyle; I had to grieve the death of the future I had once imagined. I was devastated.

I wrestled with a lot of guilt and shame over past decisions. The Lord had been an integral part of my life growing up, yet I chose to become unequally yoked with a man of a different faith. I convinced myself that God somehow got it wrong on this one, but as time passed and I walked in my faith, I realized that God never gets it wrong.

After my divorce, most people just reinforced my misery by speculating on the cause of our divorce or commenting on the negative dynamic—some even asked me why it took me so long to end it. To avoid the stinging commentary, I retreated for a long time into a dark hole where I couldn't move and where God's light had a difficult time reaching me.

Only the Word was able to bring me back out of that dark place. Ironically, my former husband had given me a Bible for Christmas just a few months before our separation.

comma where God has a period, we find trouble. Is God saying to you, *Behold, I will do a new thing.… Shall you not know it?* [Isa43:19] Are you stalled in one season of your life while God is trying to move you forward to a new thing? Every time He tries to urge you on, are you looking back longingly at where you were before, unwilling to make the move? He can't do much for you in that situation. Either He will

I put it to good use! Reading and rereading His promises and words of comfort helped rebuild my shattered self-esteem. I knew that even in my current state, I was still precious in God's sight. Remembering the depth of His love for me helped me see that I still had potential. I let Him begin to do a new thing in me.

But before I could fully enter into my best future, I had to let go of my shame over my past choices. Three things helped me do this: (1) I fell in love with the Lord and let His redeeming unconditional love heal me; (2) I cut out everything in life that did not move me toward the new future that I was trying to create (including people); (3) I began to make decisions and do things that were consistent with the Word of God, such as walking in integrity so that no new shame could enter into my life and undo the work that was being done.

My life is not what I would have imagined twenty years ago, but I know that our ways and our thoughts are lower than His, so I don't look back—I look up. The past has no more possibilities, but the future has many wonderful things in store. They begin when we quit looking back.

wait until you're ready, or He will look elsewhere for someone who is. Keep asking yourself: Where am I? Where is God trying to take me? How will I get there? What must I do to get ready to go? His plans for us are always good.^seeRom8:28 We need to hop to it, excitedly, when we see God moving!

As I (Chris) noted in Rule 3, I had to leave behind the plan *I* had for my future when God called me to leave my finance job to go to Bible school. I had to change my attitude about leaving the big city for a small town and see the value of taking this next step with God. If I had spent my time in the classroom in Oklahoma thinking about all the money I could be making on a trading floor in New York (not to mention all the free Knicks tickets!), it never would have worked.

Lot's wife was not mentally prepared for the future God had for her. She had no new wineskin in which to put the fresh new wine God wanted to give her.^seeMatt9:17

Sometimes God shuts down our relationships or careers because He has to literally chase us out or we just wouldn't go! If Pharaoh hadn't chased after the Israelites, they might not have hightailed it out of Egypt into their Promised Land. Don't miss the new thing because you are still in love with the old. The Lord is asking, "Why are you still crying over what I shut off from you?" What a shame if God is giving you an opportunity, whether it be at work, in ministry, or with a new person, and like Lot's wife, you keep looking back.

LIVING IN THE PROMISED LAND

One of Jesus's favorite disciples and friends, Peter, made a colossal blunder. He denied knowing Christ three times. As the rooster crowed he realized his sin, and *he went out and wept bitterly.*^{Matt26:75} But he didn't stay in that state, licking his wounds and lamenting the past to anyone who walked by. Why? Because Jesus, inimitable leader that He was, restored Peter's self-confidence and hope. When He appeared to the disciples after His resurrection, He specifically asked for Peter and included him in the barbecued breakfast He made for the disciples on the shores of the Sea of Tiberias.^{seeJohn21:12-15} Renewed and freed of guilt, Peter could now see that his future was still bright—in fact, brighter than it was before.

God wants to redeem and restore us from our past relationship blunders in the same way. How do we experience this renewal? By allowing Him to help us eat, drink, sleep, and think Promised Land. Here are some how-to specifics:

- *Give your regrets to Jesus Christ and leave them there.* When I (Chris) was a little boy, I was always cutting myself playing sports or running around in the yard. My mom would take the Band-Aid off after a while, put peroxide on the cut, and let it air out. "Things that are covered don't heal well," she'd say. Christ went to the cross to help us overcome the regrets of our past, but only when we humble ourselves, bring them into the light, and ask for His help do we find total healing for the pain in our soul. If you have been living in the Land of Regret, pray: *Lord, I confess that I cannot handle this. I have tried on my own to bury these thoughts and to drown them out in endless ways. But nothing is working. I am hereby relinquishing all rights to handling this on my own and I'm giving them to You. Show me what to do.* Then watch God's mercy and faithfulness begin to work for you.

- *Start memorizing scriptures that address the pain of your past.*
  This will add clarity to the bright picture of where God is
  taking you. Some good ones to remind yourself that the past
  is past include Isaiah 65:17, Luke 9:62, and Philippians 3:13.
  To know that your future is bright if you press forward, read
  Joshua 1:7, Isaiah 61, Jeremiah 1:12, and Joel 2:28.
- *Keep a journal of things God was showing you about His plan
  and destiny for your life.* In Rule 3 we encouraged you to
  keep a journal. If you have not done this, commit to doing
  so now. God has implanted in each of us a picture of what
  He wants to accomplish through us and in us. Keeping a
  journal is crucial because you will need something other
  than your circumstances to remind you of His plan for your
  life. If you don't have a written description, the vision may
  not seem real in light of your current problems or your past
  errors.

      International Bible teacher Derek Prince tells the won-
  derful story of meeting his wife, Ruth, in their book *God Is
  a Matchmaker.* In it, he describes the vision God gave him,
  showing Ruth in a certain green dress, sitting in the middle
  of a road. He knew instinctively that God was saying he was
  to marry her. At the time, he had only met her once or
  twice. But she showed up for their next meeting in the exact
  green dress she had worn in his vision! Even so, when Derek
  began to tell people about his plans, he "realized how much
  of it was subjective and supernatural. To me it was all so real
  and vivid. To others it could easily appear farfetched and fan-
  ciful."[8] So might yours if you don't write down the vision.

If we will faithfully and prayerfully take these steps, we will begin to look into the face of our Father when we're tempted by voices from the Land of Regret or the Island of Glory. We will see that our hope and our help come from Him alone. And that, yes, God still does have a great plan for your life. Let's decide once and for all that He is trustworthy and able to present us *faultless before the presence of His glory with exceeding joy*[Jude24] and to *do exceedingly abundantly above all that we ask or think.*[Eph3:20]

GET TOGETHER

We know you're asking, "Are we there yet?" But while it's exciting to sit in a new car, enjoying the aroma of the leather and fooling with all the gadgets, you won't achieve lifelong love with just a nice seat warmer. In this section, we explore how to get past the bells and whistles while courting, and we offer practical tools for securing the lasting, Christ-centered relationship you've been longing to have.

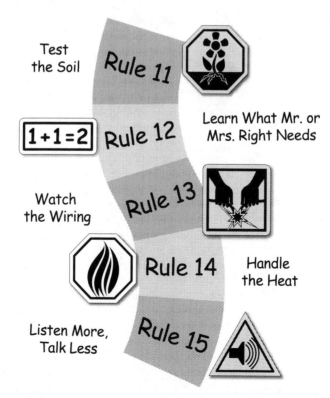

Test the Soil — Rule 11

1 + 1 = 2 — Rule 12 — Learn What Mr. or Mrs. Right Needs

Watch the Wiring — Rule 13

Rule 14 — Handle the Heat

Listen More, Talk Less — Rule 15

Test the Soil

Other seed fell on good ground and yielded a crop.

—MARK 4:8

At this point in our lives, we're looking for our lifelong soul mates—not playmates, boy toys, needy children, or surrogate mothers. So when we meet someone who smells like they could possibly someday become a potential candidate for our Mr. or Mrs. Right, we need to shut down "the giddies" and check out his or her character objectively. This is also a good time to give ourselves the once-over to see how well we've done our own prep work.

Let's take what we've learned about the mistakes of our past and resolve not to spend more of our precious time with people who are not good for us. Rest in the truth that as we grow in the things of God and practice His rules for choosing Mr. or Mrs. Right, we will attract like-minded, godly people. Testing the soil will give us the feedback we need to make the second biggest decision of our lives—whom to marry.

DIG DEEP

The parable of the sower, which appears in the books of Matthew, Mark, and Luke, contains some helpful principles for evaluating a person's character and spiritual commitment. In this story, Jesus talks about a farmer who plants seeds in four types of soil. Some soils receive the seed, which grows quickly; others receive the seed, but it doesn't take; and still other soils have the seed plucked out of them

Living It Out: Tyra's Story

At first Tyra was attracted to James because, in addition to being good-looking, he served his church as an usher and faithfully attended a weekly Bible study. Their relationship progressed nicely, and soon they were a fixture at Christian socials.

As she got to know him better, however, Tyra began noticing some incongruencies between James's talk and his behavior. When she pointed them out, he told her, "Give me some grace—I'm trying to strengthen my walk with God." His couched responses appeased her eager heart. *The man is trying,* she reasoned. *What more can I ask for?* When she asked him why he didn't seem to want to go to church with her, he told her that he wanted to be sure she was "the one" before he introduced her to all of his church buddies. When he finally did agree to visit her church, she was thrilled. He showed up, well dressed with his Bible and notebook in hand—forty minutes late. Tyra was irritated. She thought it was odd when he told her he "wasn't that into worship singing" and only wanted to hear the sermon, but she overlooked it. Later on at brunch, he expressed his love for Tyra and told her that he sensed that God was smiling on their relationship.

One night after the weekly Bible study they attended, he

almost before it's planted. Jesus then interprets the meaning of the parable, saying that the seed represents the Word of God, and the soils represent the different responses people have to the Word.

coyly suggested they pick up some take-out and go back to his apartment. When she questioned whether that was a good idea or not—after all they had just been to a Bible study on holiness—he laughed it off and told her he had something important to tell her that needed "just the right setting." Excited, Tyra accompanied him back to his house. Over the third glass of wine, arms intertwined, he whispered between sips, "Ty, you really are the perfect woman for me. You have a great relationship with God and you're beautiful. I like that. Marriage is definitely on my mind. But God knows a man has certain needs and...the Bible says He understands our weaknesses. We could test the waters a little bit before we commit to engagement." His question, "What do you think?" got lost in the sultry kisses he was planting on Tyra's perfumed neck. She *didn't* think.

In the background, Tyra could hear her PM screaming, "Noooooooo!" She heard, but she didn't listen. With the mood set, Tyra ended up staying far into the night. The two were soon parking at each other's apartments often, especially on Saturday nights (to make it more convenient to attend church together on Sunday morning). Tyra began to experience a "low-grade guilt" but continued to "make the best of a bad situation" for the next two years. Finally, the two parted company—hurt, angry, and disillusioned.

Here's how *The Message* translates the story:

*The farmer plants the Word. Some people are like the seed that falls on **the hardened soil of the road.** No sooner do they hear the Word than Satan snatches away what has been planted in them.*

    *And some are like the seed that lands **in the gravel.** When they first hear the Word, they respond with great enthusiasm. But there is such shallow soil of character that when the emotions wear off and some difficulty arrives, there is nothing to show for it.*

    *The seed cast **in the weeds** represents the ones who hear the kingdom news but are overwhelmed with worries about all the things they have to do and all the things they want to get. The stress strangles what they heard, and nothing comes of it.*

    *But the seed planted **in the good earth** represents those who hear the Word, embrace it, and produce a harvest beyond their wildest dreams.* Mark 4:14-20

All topsoil looks good, but often when you dig deeper you find rocks and bugs. Before you make a commitment to a person you are dating, evaluate his or her spiritual soil. Where does he or she fit in the parable?

- *The hardened soil of the road.* These are men and women whose hearts are hardened toward the things of God. They may be churchgoers, but they remain pessimistic. They belittle and question the promises of God and can quench your enthusiasm for what God is doing in your life. When you get excited about a revelation or insight you receive from a sermon or in your private devotions or weekly Bible study, they will try to make you doubt its validity. They also encourage you to compromise your moral values and live a nominal Christian life.

- *The seed that lands in the gravel.* These individuals get excited when they hear about "spiritual things," but when the Christian life begins to cost them something, they make comments like, "I don't know about this Christianity thing." They give a church offering but are skeptical about tithing. They only give when it's convenient and money is in abundance. (They have cirrhosis of the giver!) They come to church late or leave early; their attitude is "just the sermon please." They read the Bible occasionally but talk more about Dr. Phil or Iyanla Vanzant's advice. They discourage you from other-than-Sunday commitments to your faith and jump at the chance to skip church to do something "more fun."

- *The seed cast in the weeds.* People in this category appreciate God but tend to have a value system driven by money and promotion. Whenever they have to choose between God and money, money wins. They will move to another state because of a higher paying job with little concern about leaving the church that was feeding them spiritually. Because they view time as money, they spend most of it trying to make more cash, and thus have little time to spend with God, in Bible studies, with Christian friends (or with you!). They serve their church community, which they regard as a social steppingstone, by sending a large annual check; they have little desire for personal involvement in ministry. Their best friends are often their unsaved business associates or their fraternity or sorority buddies.

- *The seed planted in the good earth.* These men and women share your love for the Lord and seek after the things of God. Their walk is consistent with their talk. They are the same people when they are in a group Bible study as they are when they are out to dinner with friends, at their family's house, or on the phone with you. As you share your struggles and victories in the faith, you receive encouragement and feedback from their own Christ-centered wellspring. Such people have the potential to be an equal yoke.

It is our opinion that you should not invest much time trying to court someone who is on the wayside, covered in gravel, or stuck in the weeds. This person just isn't ready, and you don't know when, or if, he or she ever will be. If you recognize yourself in one of the first three soils, by all means turn to page 69, pray the Lordship Prayer, and get rooted!

WAIT FOR ROOTS TO GROW

Note this: Being equally yoked spiritually doesn't mean being equally *mature* spiritually. If a person is truly "good ground," he or she will continue to grow spiritually and that growth will be tangible. So, to be sure that the person you are dating is truly good ground, check his or her spiritual growth rate. People who are serious about God have few inconsistencies in their walk and talk—and when incongruencies are pointed out, they don't excuse them. Instead, they repent and ask their PM to help them change in those areas.

The Bible describes Christian growth—called sanctification—as an individual process that happens in stages. It's not a one-time event. Consider these verses:

For the earth yields crops by itself: first the blade, then the head, after that the full grain in the head. Mark 4:28

For precept must be upon precept…line upon line, line upon line, here a little, there a little. Isa 28:10

For in it the righteousness of God is revealed from faith to faith. Rom 1:17

But we all…are being transformed into the same image from glory to glory, just as by the Spirit of the Lord. 2 Cor 3:18

Even if you have met your Mr. or Mrs. Right, don't assume that you will grow spiritually in the same areas at the same pace. One person may be more astute in a certain area than the other. Making Jesus Lord of your life is the event you both have in common, but working out your salvation is a process that each of you undergo at your own pace. see Phil 2:12

Jesus referred to this when He said, *Other seed fell on good ground and yielded a crop that sprang up, increased and produced: some thirtyfold, some sixty, and some a hundred.* Mark 4:8 While the seeds that fell on the good ground all produced something, notice that some produced more than others.

Only you can decide whether the pace and quality of Mr. or Mrs.

Good Ground's growth is in line with reasonable expectations and your personal, God-inspired time line. Make sure this person is teachable and eager to grow deeper roots. Be patient and watch carefully to see if your potential mate is demonstrating the fruit of the Spirit.

As you examine whether Mr. or Mrs. Good Ground is the real deal, it's necessary to examine both *what* you hear and *how* you hear.

USE HEARING AIDS

How's your hearing when it comes to your relationship? Jesus said to the disciples, *Take heed **what** you hear...and to you who hear, more will be given.*Mark 4:24

Ask yourself these questions:

- What am I hearing from my Personal Mentor about this person?
- Does something continue to nag at my conscience about his or her character?
- What do my parents or trusted relatives say? (Like it or not, they have lived a lot more life than we have. Even if they have not made the best decisions, they often have tremendous insight from their own mistakes.)
- What do my closest friends and trusted counselors say? Have they raised issues that I continue to sweep under the carpet?

Luke records, *Therefore take heed **how** you hear. For whoever has, to him more will be given; and whoever does not have, even what he seems to have will be taken from him.*8:18

In the beginning of a relationship, we are often so infatuated with each other that we can't hear anything but love songs. Time, patience, and self-control work together to help a healthy, godly relationship to progress. We need to allow for just enough of each to calm those "giddies" so that we can make wise decisions about whether and how to move forward.

Ask yourself these questions:

- Am I listening with an open heart to how the person's character and behavior reflect the teachings of Christ?
- Am I sensitive to what my spirit is saying versus my heart? Am I allowing the Word to be the divider between the two?
- When I reach a "fork in the road" and feel unrest, do I follow after peace?
- Am I listening as I spend time with the person? Or am I so "in love with being in love" that infatuation has clouded my judgment?

Now that you've asked yourself the important questions, it's time to evaluate where this person stands on some specific issues. To do this, ask:

- Does this person respect my commitment to the things of God?
- Does this person cause me to live a more morally pure life or a less morally pure life?
- Does this person belittle my attempts to please the Lord?
- How does this person interact with his or her family? friends?
- Is the person naturally negative or positive?
- Does this person embrace the plan that I believe God has called me to do?
- Whom does this person allow to speak into his or her life? Does the person accept godly counsel?

- Does this person respond with true remorse when he or she has hurt or offended me?
- Does this person have an accurate perspective of his or her weaknesses? Is this person endeavoring to fix them?

Chris and Pam's Qualities of a Good-Soil Date

- God is glorified in all aspects of the date: location, conversation, and conduct.
- Both people are dressed attractively and modestly, not trying to seduce or entice. (When in doubt, ask an elderly lady how you look before you go out!)
- The setting is conducive to getting to know the other person, without competing elements like a movie or sports event (at least for the first several dates).
- The person expresses more interest in finding out about you than in telling you about him- or herself.
- The person talks freely about his or her parents and siblings.
- Your conversation is consistent with godly values.
- You do not observe any neuroses (obvious anxieties or phobias) or clear character flaws.
- The other person does not attempt to violate any boundaries that you set up, physically or emotionally.
- After the date, you don't feel any "low-grade guilt" because of the way you conducted yourself.
- The date doesn't last all night.

- Does this person enjoy an environment that is conducive to the things of God or to the things of the world?
- How has this person described his or her previous relationships? Does this individual always blame the other person, or does he or she assume personal responsibility for part of the problem?

If you have experienced divorce, also ask:

- Is this person empathetic to my deeply wounded areas?
- Does he or she understand the "fear of abandonment" or other such issues I might have in getting remarried?
- Is this person willing to undergird me during the healing process I must undergo?
- Does this person have a commitment to my children?
- Does the person understand and agree with my financial commitment to my children, and possibly to my former spouse?
- Does this person have the same expectations as I do about having children if we get married?

While answering these questions and following "good date" rules can seem cumbersome, it is critical to helping you find God's intended mate for you. Besides, you don't want to duplicate what happened to David when he saw Bathsheba. He was a good man in a bad place in a weak moment. Without the proper boundaries and the right information on Mr. or Mrs. Good Ground, you too may be a person after God's own heart who slips into the Enemy's snare.

But fear not: God's rules are here to help you.

Learn What Mr. or Mrs. Right Needs

Study to shew thyself approved.

—2 Timothy 2:15, KJV

One primary cause of problems in relationships is that we don't understand, appreciate, and celebrate the different ways God made His sons and daughters. Women persist in writing men fourteen-page love letters and sending them cards and daisies at the office, and men continue to purchase household appliances and dime-store trinkets for their girlfriends or wives on Valentine's Day.

It is way past time to get over this mountain so we can live long and prosper—together! To do so, we need to understand these five simple truths:

1. Men and women are different.
2. Most of us give the person we're courting or dating what *we* need instead of what *he* or *she* needs.
3. Doing this causes frustration in the relationship and may lead to unnecessary breakup.
4. What a husband needs most from a wife is respect.
5. What a wife needs most from a husband is love.

Let's explore each of these and then discuss tangible ways you can acquire specific information on the needs of *your* potential Mr. or Mrs. Right.

MEN AND WOMEN ARE DIFFERENT

Everything between you two seemed to be going along just fine, when
suddenly you hit a mysterious sour note:

"I don't know why she suddenly became so quiet at dinner."

"I can't believe he wasn't thrilled by my surprise visit."

"Why on earth did he say *that?*"

"She didn't even want to talk to me. What did I do?"

Zhis is ze beginning of ze frustrashun. Your love interest is not
responding to you the way you think he or she "should." What often
follows are judgmental attitudes, condescending remarks, and negative behaviors that shoot intimacy in the foot. If this tension escalates,
the relationship might end right there, when it doesn't necessarily
need to. Sadly, a lot of marriages end right there, too, when they didn't
need to. So before you marry, do some prevention. Peruse this list of
male and female differences, which we have adapted from *Understanding Love* by Dr. Myles Munroe:[1]

IN GENERAL, MEN...	IN GENERAL, WOMEN...
• are logical thinkers	• are emotional feelers
• speak in order to express their thoughts	• speak in order to express their feelings
• listen in order to receive information	• listen for the emotions being expressed
• take things impersonally	• tend to take things personally
• are interested in the prin-ciple, the abstract, or the philosophy	• are interested in the details

IN GENERAL, MEN…	IN GENERAL, WOMEN…
• want to know how to get there (in material things)	• tend to look at the goal only (in material things)
• focus on the goal (in spiritual or intangible things)	• want to know how to get there (in spiritual or intangible things)
• have a mind like a filing cabinet	• have a mind like a computer [multitaskers]
• view their job as an extension of their personality	• view home as an extension of their personality
• are nomadic	• need security and roots
• tend to be more resentful than women	• tend to be guilt prone
• are emotionally stable	• are always changing
• tend to stand back and evaluate before they get involved	• tend to be involved more easily and more quickly than men
• need to be told things again and again	• never forget
• tend to remember the gist of things rather than the details	• tend to remember the details and sometimes distort the gist

We can see from this list the broad contrasts between men and women. Educate yourself on how you and the person you hope to court may be different by doing a careful, item-by-item comparison. (Remember, waiting is all about preparing, not sitting passively, hoping Mr. or Mrs. Right will fall from the sky.)

Often we just coast along in a relationship, assuming that the other person will see things the way we do. (After all, we're so in love!) Nothing could more untrue. No one changes his or her nature that much. By arming yourself with a clear understanding of the basic differences in the opposite sex, you will gain invaluable insights that will help you minimize frustration and maximize communication.

We Give the Other Person What We Need Most Instead of What He or She Needs Most

Why do so many of us walk around frustrated in relationships? The simple answer is that most people we interact with have not discovered how to meet our needs—no one has cared enough to find out what they are. Consequently, our default button is to return the same treatment—just as we did in the school yard. "She hit me, so I hit her back," we told the teacher. We grow up, get into relationships, and say, "You don't meet my needs, I won't meet yours." What happened to esteeming the other person as greater than yourself?[seePhil2:3] It may sound corny, but God set this rule in place just so we'd have fabulous relationships.

Many men often confuse deeds with needs. They think that as long as they're doing *things* for a woman, her needs must be getting met. (Because men are wired to *do*.) So a frustrated husband will say, "I cut the grass. I took out the garbage. *Whaddaya want?*" A boyfriend might say, "I don't look at other women. I take you to nice places. I'm not pressuring you for sex. *Whaddaya want?*" Meanwhile, a woman needs to hear, "I love you. I'm glad to see you. Your new haircut looks great." She needs *her person* to be affirmed. A boyfriend may give a woman space when she's under pressure at the office and has an exam after work. He won't call because he doesn't want to disturb her. What he doesn't know is that she is sitting at her desk feeling unloved because on her most pressurized day, she isn't hearing him say, "I just called to tell you you're wonderful, I'm praying for you, and everything is going to turn out fine."

According to studies of married couples in *His Needs, Her Needs* by Willard Harley Jr., most women want conversation from their husbands even more than financial security or family commitment. Most men need their wives to be a recreational companion even more than they need her to be beautiful or to provide them with a clean house and nice meals.[2] Women often want closeness while men want activity and adventure. (Sexual fulfillment is first on Harley's list for men, but that's for another book.)

If we keep trying to meet the other person's needs in ways that are meaningful to *us* rather than to them, we keep the circle of unmet needs going round and round. A successful (happy) marriage depends upon each partner's ability to meet the top emotional need of the other person. This requires identifying those top needs and anticipating them. To do this, take note of these things in your potential Mr. or Mrs. Right:

- What things does he or she ask for *repeatedly*? (Examples include more time on the phone or time spent together, less time on the phone or spent together, a date night every week, a walk in the park, that you wear less makeup, that you "look nice" more often, a relationship update every month, that you support him or her at sporting events, in ministry, and so on.)
- Ask, "What makes your day feel complete?"
- Observe: What causes a noticeable change in his or her countenance or disposition?

- Ask, "What specific things make deposits and withdrawals into your emotional account?" (Read: make you feel satisfied and happy versus unsatisfied and unhappy.)

James 4:2 says, *You do not have because you do not ask.* You will not know what your potential Mr. or Mrs. Right needs if you never ask or intentionally take the time to observe him or her. Ask yourself the same questions above, and jot down some notes on yourself. The more you know about your own needs, the better you'll be able to communicate them. Most of us just sit back and expect those we love to get an A+ in Mind Reading. Most never do, which again results in unmet needs.

God is the only mind reader. He paid the price for the sin He *foreknew* we would commit and sent a Savior to redeem us *before* we knew we needed one!^{seeIsa65:24} Your mate is not God. It takes work to understand and meet each other's needs, but just think of the wonderful climate we could create in our relationships if we did!

IF WE CONTINUE TO GIVE THE OTHER PERSON WHAT WE NEED INSTEAD OF WHAT HE OR SHE NEEDS, THE END RESULT WILL BE FRUSTRATION

What we don't know can't hurt us, right? Wrong. The Bible tells us that we are destroyed because of ignorance, because we reject knowledge.^{seeHos4:6} Ignorance in any capacity is not something to be taken lightly and shrugged off.

Unmet needs and empty emotional accounts cause relationships to break down—even if you are a spiritual giant. Our needs motivate our behavior, and we will go to great lengths to have those needs met. If they are not met, we won't function properly. To explain this bet-

ter, we'll use the analogy of a computer operating system. Most operating systems have windows that are used to view various programs.
In the upper-right-hand corner of the screen is a small *X* icon. When
we click on it, the window shuts down or closes. We no longer have
access to it. A similar thing can happen when our emotional needs are
not being met in a relationship. The windows of our soul (mind, will,
and emotions) start to shut down. While it's easy to reopen a window
on a computer, it's not easy to reopen our soul once we have shut it
down in a relationship. So, in computer language, when your potential Mr. or Mrs. Right's screen is flashing: ARE YOU SURE YOU WANT
[ME] TO SHUT DOWN? be afraid. Be very afraid. Go back and answer
the above questions so that those emotional needs can be met before
the screen goes black. As you diligently practice what you learn, your
relationship frustrations will decrease dramatically.

Pay close attention to these next two points so you can be armed
with the basic understanding of what (most) men and women need
most.

A Husband Needs to Be Shown Respect and Admiration

The major interstate on the map to Mr. Right's heart is Respect Road,
and the primary way a woman can demonstrate her respect for her
man is through words. A woman's words have considerable power to
affect the climate of a relationship and a home. She can use words to
encourage her husband or to deflate him, to create a calm atmosphere
or a tense one, to make him feel like a king or like a fool. In other
words, she's one powerful woman!

Give Him Peace

Most men view life through a peace continuum. In their relationships, men want to lengthen the peace line into the next minute, the next hour, the next day, and so on. This is one reason men will do anything to avoid confrontation. (The other is that they are just afraid!) As we're sure you've noticed, a man tends to withdraw in discussions that he deems...um...threatening. Most men shrink from conversations that begin with, "We need to talk"—especially when these words are accompanied by a frown, a hand on the hip, or folded arms.

Wives-in-training: It's all about presentation, presentation, presentation. You will get a more positive response if you *ask,* "When can we talk about ——?" (with no threatening body language). You may have something valid to say, something *God* wants you to say, but a poor or untimely presentation may cause it to be delayed for two weeks or two years. If the King of kings stands at the door and knocks before He comes in,[seeRev3:20] what makes us think we can just barge into someone's thoughts anytime we want?

Other words that rob a man's peace and can cause him to emotionally shut down include negative comments that start with "You never..." or "You always..." Remember, only Satan is the accuser.[seeRev12:10] You are not to be an agent of the Enemy in your future mate's life! Strike these phrases from your vocabulary. No good comes of them.

It also costs a man peace when a woman asks him rhetorical questions. Here are some examples:

- Do you really think that waffle iron you gave me was a good birthday gift?
- Do you truly think I'm prettier than she is?

And the clincher:

• Do you honestly think you love me as much as I love you?

When you use words like *really, truly,* and *honestly,* you automatically imply that he's lied about something he told you, and who wants to be accused of that (especially when he hasn't eaten yet and the game's about to come on)? Plus, it's just plain unattractive and comes across as insecure. If our security is in Christ, we shouldn't need to ask these questions—and certainly not in a coy and deceptive manner. Men like directness, so if you want to know if you look good to him, simply ask, "How do I look?" and be ready to handle the answer.

What can a wife-in-training do when a man does something that troubles her? God's Word says, *In the same way, you wives, be submissive to your own husbands so that even if any of them are disobedient to the word, they may be won without a word by the behavior of their wives, as they observe your chaste and respectful behavior.*[1Pet3:1-2NASB] Hold on. The phrase *without a word* does not mean a wife has to tiptoe around with pursed lips. It means that she blesses her husband immensely when she chooses not to nag, fuss, or pout to get her point across. A wise woman will pick her relationship battles and then win them with her godly countenance and self-controlled tongue. In so doing, she will show a man she respects him. Again, for a man, the less drama the better.

If you don't believe us, read these wise sayings from Proverbs about the joys of living with a contentious woman (all written by a man—Solomon):

Better to dwell in the wilderness, than with a contentious and angry woman.[21:19]

It is better to dwell in a corner of a housetop, than in a house shared with a contentious woman.[25:24]

A continual dripping on a very rainy day, and a contentious woman are alike.[27:15]

A man will often avoid interaction if he fears that the conversation will bring him only criticism and condemnation (read: more drama). Men need to find a safe, peaceful place in their wives; they need them to be a cushion where they can lay their heads and rest after a hard day. Is that you?

Cheer Him On

Men will always gravitate toward the loudest applause. That's why they gravitate toward the softball league, the men's meeting, the gym, or the happy hour. It's why some keep reliving bygone days when they were the star of their football team and why others have to be pried away from their desks. They simply want to be in the place where they get the biggest cheers and the most frequent pats on the back.

Never allow anyone to cheer more loudly for your man than you. I (Pam) didn't realize how important this was to guys. In fact, I was embarrassed one night when I heard myself yelling a boyfriend's name at a basketball game as he dribbled down court—that is, until the night he came to me teary-eyed and told me he heard my voice above the roar of the crowd. First Peter 3:2 tells wives, *You are to feel for him all that reverence includes: to respect, defer to, revere him—to honor, esteem, appreciate, prize, and...adore him, that is, to admire, praise, be devoted to, deeply love, and enjoy your husband.*[AMP] *Selah.*

One reason men need to hear praise is that it helps them "keep score." As linear thinkers, men naturally gravitate toward objectives that are quantifiable. They like to know how they are doing, what the stats are in a relationship. This is why many men run after money, promotions, or possessions: quantifiable things. It's difficult for a man to know how he's doing in a romantic relationship. How does he keep score? When he feels he is not making progress, or the scorecard seems nebulous or constantly fluctuating, a man has a tendency to stop try- ing. This is why respect and admiration from a woman are so impor- tant. Your gift of continual encouragement and respect helps him know he's doing okay in the relationship.

Wives-in-training, don't let your husband-to-be feel he has a los- ing stat sheet with you—especially if he's enjoying winning stats at work. Comfort and encourage him with your smile and your words. When you do that consistently, he puts a mental plus mark on the Relationship Stat Sheet.

Make Him Feel Like a King

Every man has a king and a fool inside of him, and whichever his princess speaks to is usually who will emerge. Men long to find women who know how to bring out the greatness in them—the king within—through their words and encouragement.

First Samuel 25 tells the story of a wise woman who lived out this truth. Here's an extreme paraphrase: When King David was traveling in the desert, he heard about a wealthy man named Nabal. David and his men were hungry and in need of supplies, so he sent some men to ask Nabal if he could give them some food, which was a customary request in their culture. Nabal not only refused, he was rude about it.

This foolish man angered King David because he didn't show the respect he was due. Only through the intervention of Nabal's wife, Abigail, and her ability to placate David's wrath, did the story end well. Abigail calmed her churlish husband and praised David with grace and style. She reminded him that his short-term retribution toward Nabal could cause him to forfeit his God-given destiny and assignment.

This powerful biblical story teaches the power of a woman who knows how to communicate with a man. The Bible says that Abigail had good understanding or intelligence and a beautiful countenance.[1Sam25:3] Incidentally, the word *countenance* comes from the root word *contain*. This woman was not only physically attractive and poised, but she also knew how to contain her tongue! She was able to recognize godly traits in a man (even though she was married to a man who didn't possess them). Abigail was respectful and kind to David and made him feel like the king he was. Because she did, he did not kill her husband or ransack their household—and she did all of this without a low-cut blouse or a high-cut skirt. Ten days later God struck Nabal dead, and King David asked Abigail to be his wife. (Not a bad deal.)

One way you can make your Mr. Right feel like a king is by allowing him to lead the relationship. He may be so shocked at first that he won't know exactly what to do, but a man after God's heart will learn quickly. If he can't handle being "king" of the relationship—he's not ready for marriage! We said earlier that being king and prophet in a relationship means taking the lead and executing a vision for the relationship. That means he needs to study your vulnerabilities as a couple and then take steps to ensure that you stay on course. For some couples, late-night phone calls may be a no-no, for others it may be the tendency to overspend on dates. Perhaps sexy music or romantic ballads set your minds and bodies adrift. It is the man's responsibility before God to steward, or care for, the woman and direct the relationship. As he does this in courtship, he is preparing for the same role in marriage.

Timing Is Everything

Sometimes timing makes the difference between a word being received as good counsel and a word being received as nagging. Be selective about when you approach a man to have The Talk. While it's important for women, who are emotional feelers, to keep their communication account current, men, who are logical thinkers, want to process things first. That's why after pouring out their hearts for an hour countless women plead, "Don't you have anything to say?" only to have him respond, "No, not really."

Encouraging Word

*Death and life are in the power of the tongue.*Prov18:21

If a neutral third party eavesdropped on your last conversation with your potential mate, what would he or she conclude? Who came out in the interaction, the king or the fool?

Queen Esther knew something about timing. She fasted for three days before she went before the king with her request. (And she fed him twice before she asked!)seeEsther4–5 So, wives-in-training, pray about the timing if you're about to drop a bomb on your potential mate. State your case succinctly, with a minimum of emotion, and then give him time to process what you've said before you require a response. You'll be happier with the result!

A WIFE NEEDS TO BE SHOWN LOVE AND AFFECTION

Women have longed for love and relationships since the beginning of time. When Eve entered the world, the first thing she knew was a relationship—with Adam. Perhaps that's why women tend to be more relationship-oriented than men. Bachelor boy Adam knew how to count and name animals, tend a garden, and walk with God, but he wasn't skilled in giving love to another human being until Eve came along.

Husbands-in-training, what your future Mrs. Right needs from you is your love. She may often ask herself, "I wonder if he really loves me?" She needs the security of knowing she's loved by you. In truth, as a man *leave[s] his father and his mother, and shall cleave unto his wife,*[Gen2:24KJV] his love and loyalty should provide an even greater sense of security for her than she had when she was with her parents. Nothing can harm a woman's confidence more than a husband who's not dependable. She relies on him to be her lover (an affectionate and benevolent friend; someone devoted to only her).

While there are no scriptures that tell women explicitly to love their husbands,[3] Ephesians 5 tells husbands three times to make sure they love their wives:

> *Husbands, love your wives, just as Christ also loved the church and gave Himself for her.... So husbands ought to love their own wives as their own bodies; he who loves his wife loves him-*

self.… Nevertheless let each one of you in particular so love his own wife as himself, and let the wife see that she respects her husband.[vv25,28,33]

Why the repetition? We think it's because women are lovers and nurturers, and they want to be loved back. Thus, it is crucial that a man learn how to show a woman love, and to do so in a way that she can receive it. If she was abused early in life, a woman may have a difficult time receiving that love, but God instills the desire in every female. A husband's unconditional love can help cover and draw out his wife's hidden treasure in this area. (Rereading Rule 5 can help too.)

Speak Her Love Language

Note that we said a husband should love his wife *in a way that she can receive it.* Until a woman is loved in a way that touches her soul (her mind, will, and emotions), her emotional account will remain low. As we stated previously, men often confuse activities with needs. If a wife receives love best through encouraging words, and her husband never compliments her or only tells her that he loves her on their anniversary, she will feel frustrated. When she expresses this frustration, he repeats a long laundry list of *activities* that he is doing for her, unaware that he still is not meeting her need to feel loved by him.

We believe it's godly for a man to speak words of love to a woman he is engaged to marry. (It's defrauding to do this earlier, when there's no firm commitment.) She wants to be loved in her language. *Parlez-vous?* Find out if it's words, cards, flowers, acts of service, or hand-holding she needs to feel loved—and then meet that need. As a man develops true intimacy with God, he gains sensitivity about how he can love his future wife better. For more on intimacy with God, go back and reread Rule 4.

Empathize with Her

Ephesians 5 exhorts husbands to love their wives as Christ loves the church. It notes that He gave Himself *that He might present her to Himself...not having spot or wrinkle...and without blemish.*[Eph5:27]

Let's consider that the *spots* in a woman's life are the challenges she faces from the outside world. The source might be pressure from work, school, or from societal stereotypes about women. A *wrinkle* in her life might symbolize some internal decay. A wife wants her husband to hear her angst about the spots and wrinkles in her life and to offer empathy and comfort. Perhaps your girlfriend's spot is the fact that she's underpaid and overworked, and she needs you to compliment the efforts she makes in the relationship as a way to help compensate for that—she wants to feel valuable to you. Or her wrinkle may be the fact that she was never allowed to give her opinion in her home growing up, so she needs you to show that you want her input and include her in decision making.

How can you do this? By allowing her to use as many words as she needs to express how she is feeling when she's experiencing hardship. This can be extremely challenging, because you may feel that she is talking in circles when you want her to talk in a straight line. (There's that linear thinker versus emotional thinker again!) Do it anyway. Resist every temptation to interrupt when this is happening. Cut a woman off once when she's trying to share something deep and emotional with you, and watch the climate change. To avoid the deep freeze, before the conversation starts, ask whether this is a "Give me an answer" talk or a "Just hear me out" talk. This way you can avoid your natural tendency to dissect and solve if she just wants a sympathetic ear and a hug.

I (Pam) used to conduct reconciliation groups with Christians of different ethnicities. We had a rule that whenever anyone was speaking, everyone else in the group was to listen without interrupting or trying to reinterpret the person's story. Without this respect, the person talking often felt like his or her experience was being invalidated. With it, the person felt heard and often received tremendous healing. The same rule applies for couples.

DON'T SKIP THIS RULE

So now you've learned that a great marriage is more than a romantic fantasy; it involves acquiring skill and proficiency in Relationship Management 101. Many married couples whose relationships failed had the desire to succeed but didn't bother to make a study of their future spouse. Men, do not say: "I'm going to skip this preparation stuff and jump to the book called *Having Better Sex in Marriage.*" You can't skip grades when you desire a godly marriage. You must graduate from each course (with at least a B).

Having a great marriage may require you to do things that are unnatural to you—listening when you want to watch television, waiting when you want to talk, just cuddling when you want to have sex. We need a paradigm shift in our thinking about what makes marriage work. Humility always precedes exaltation. Jesus exemplified this relationship principle in His life, His ministry, and especially in His death and resurrection.[seePhil2:1-11] We must humbly empty ourselves of all the misconceptions we've held about relationships and open our mind and spirit to receive truth.

As you drive toward Marriage Mountain, will you humble yourself or will you wait for the relationship to humble you?

Watch the Wiring

Can two walk together, except they be agreed?

—Amos 3:3, kjv

Psychologist and author Neil Clark Warren studied failed marriages in order to understand what went wrong and when it went wrong. His overwhelming conclusion? Incompatibility. "In almost every case, these were two persons who should never have married each other!"[4] By now you have seen the importance of spiritual compatibility within a marriage. But some compatibility in our wiring is also critical. As we learned in Rule 6, we are tripart beings, made up of spirit, soul, and body, in that order.[see 1 Thess 5:23] So we are spiritual beings, but we each have a soul and live in an earth suit called the body. According to Drs. Richard and Phyllis Arno, noted Christian psychologists, our temperaments are housed in the soul and are the inborn part of us that determines how we react to people, places, and things. "Happiness in marriage is greatly dependent on how well each spouse understands their partner's temperament and how willing they are to meet their partner's temperament needs."[5]

We should not assume that when we marry someone, his or her wiring will adapt to work with our own. As we approach engagement, we must be tuned in closely to the voice of our PM. If you are trying to close the deal and He's whispering, "Unauthorized purchase!

Unauthorized purchase!" please heed the warning. *Any enterprise is built by wise planning, becomes strong through common sense, and profits wonderfully by keeping abreast of the facts.*[Prov24:3-4TLB] As Chris's pastor always says, "We are spiritual beings mastering the human experience." When we are led by the Spirit, wisdom, common sense, and knowledge, we can make a wise choice in a mate.

It is important to study the person we are considering marrying, so we can gather information about his or her personality, interests, and lifestyles and then assess how well they will work with our own. For instance, if you're a man who loves to entertain and be around lots of people, you need to know if your potential Mrs. Right will support that—or will it be a constant drain on her energy and her nerves? If you're a woman who lives by a budget and pays her credit card bill off every month, think twice about marrying a carefree spender without considerable conversation beforehand.

Articulate your hopes, dreams, and goals, so you can be sure Mr. or Mrs. Right is on board with your God-given assignment (see Rule 3). For instance, did you know she dreams of one day opening a halfway house for drug-addicted teenagers? Or did you know that he longs to share his faith by teaching English in Japan? Life goals such as these are ideally discussed *before* marriage.

In this rule we'll examine how your potential mate's temperament and goals dovetail with your own.

What Makes You Tick?

In *Transformed Temperaments,* author Tim LaHaye used the traits of biblical characters Peter, Moses, Abraham, and Paul to illustrate the four major temperaments: Sanguine, Melancholy, Choleric, and

Phlegmatic. Some counselors also recognize a fifth temperament called Supine. Within our basic temperaments, each of us has strengths (the adorable traits you love in him or her) and weaknesses (the less adorable traits in him or her).

As we noted in Rule 12, most relationship troubles are caused by the fallout from unmet needs. People's needs change over time but not that much. Only as we submit to our Personal Mentor, the Holy Spirit, can He shape and mold us so we can exhibit more of our temperament strengths and less of the weaknesses. God gave each of us a unique design when He created us, and He wants to join us with a person who will bring out the beauty of His design in us. Though the design can get tarnished by the stuff that life piles on us, His original plan for each of us was specific and good, fearful and wonderful. So He's not going to scrap the intrinsic beauty of quiet Jane in order to have her conform to the nature of ever-ebullient Jim.

God intended for married couples to balance and complement each other as they become one. He doesn't want us to just "put up" with each other in marriage; He wants us to be yoke fellows, joined, linked as close companions, working together within a frame fitted for us.[see2Cor6:14] Can you see why it's critical that a potential Mr. or Mrs. Right fit your frame?

The temperament analysis exercise you're about to complete will help you learn about yourself and gain clarity about meeting each other's primary temperament needs.

KNOW YOUR TEMPERAMENT: AN EXERCISE

You will have a clear advantage in your relationship if you know what makes both you and your potential mate tick—and what ticks you off.

You'll gain this advantage by determining both of your temperament strengths and weaknesses. To do this, make two lists of traits that stand out in your life, positive traits on one side and negative traits on the other. Then look at the following lists and match the traits on your list with the corresponding traits to get an idea of your primary temperament and its strengths and weaknesses. Please note: This information will give you a basic idea of your temperament(s). It is not designed to identify actual behaviors, only behavior traits characteristic of that temperament. For a conclusive and in-depth description of your temperament, we suggest you take the Temperament Analysis Profile (TAP) test and review it with a trained Christian counselor. See our Recommended Reading section for where to get information on this.

As you go through this exercise, be aware that we can exhibit one temperament in public and another in private or in one-on-one settings. For example, a woman who is a life-of-the-party Sanguine could also be a withdrawn, quiet Melancholy when she's away from a crowd. After you have identified your primary temperament, see if you can identify a second, less dominant one. Which one describes your public persona? Which one describes your private persona? Have your potential mate also complete this exercise (separately), and then come together and share the information you glean.

I (Pam) was so fascinated by temperaments and their traits that I took several courses using this model and learned how to use it as a helpful tool in Christian counseling. The section that follows is based on what I learned from this model. Often, a person may spend many sessions with a counselor before he or she gets to the root of the problem. I think the Temperament Analysis Profile test helps greatly in that it provides the counselor and counselees with an accurate blueprint of their behavioral tendencies. Ideally, you would take the official TAP test and bring your findings to a counselor who is trained to explain what they mean. The counselor can help you better understand each other and can recommend strategies for maximizing each of your temperament strengths (which glorify God) and minimizing temperament weaknesses (which dishonor God).

We hope you find this temperament exercise helpful. Be sure to pray together before you begin. When you share the results, avoid accusatory statements such as, "This proves it! You are *so* stingy/insensitive/boring/careless!" Be gentle as you analyze your findings about each other—after all, you may commit to a lifetime together!

Temperament Traits

Sanguine
If many of the items on your lists match up with the following, your primary influence may be Sanguine.

Strengths	Weaknesses
cheerful	weak-willed
compassionate	undisciplined, unorganized
talkative, expressive	restless (when inactive)
enthusiastic	impulsive
charming	arrogant
inspirational	loud
friendly	rude
carefree	exaggerates
	impatient with tasks

Relationship Notes About Sanguines

They love to be around people and can feel restless and unhappy when they aren't.

On date night a Sanguine might often say: "Let's go out!"

Qualities you'll love: Inspirational with a zest for life; see the glass as half full; rarely down or depressed

Tendencies that might be difficult to deal with in marriage: May spend money carelessly; often talk without thinking first; hate housework; get easily bored and distracted; apologize sincerely but rarely change the behavior

Highest hurdles: Impetuous and impulsive; undisciplined

Heart-cry of the Sanguine: "Look at me, love me, touch me, applaud me!"

Greatest fear: Disapproval

Greatest needs in marriage might be: Frequent sex (male) or frequent cuddling, petting, and words of love (females)

Scripture to help balance fears: He made us accepted in the Beloved.[Eph1:6]

Melancholy

If many of the items on your lists match up with the following, your primary influence may be Melancholy.

Strengths	Weaknesses
	inflexible
strong-minded,	withdrawn
intellectual	self-centered
gifted	critical

loves learning

Strengths

sensitive

perfectionist

idealistic

faithful friend

persistent

self-sacrificing

Weaknesses

moody

negative

rebellious

vengeful

Relationship Notes About Melancholys

They love intimacy and can feel anxious and unhappy when forced to spend time with lots of people.

On date night a Melancholy might often say: "Let's stay in!"

Qualities you'll love: Very responsible, dependable, and loyal; idealistic, smart

Tendencies that might be difficult to deal with in marriage: Can be too critical, have a high demand for total truth, order, and reliability

Highest hurdles: Learning how to overcome negative thinking and talk; improving low self-esteem and insecurity

Heart-cry of the Melancholy: "I just need some space!"

Greatest fear: Rejection; financial instability; failure

Greatest need in marriage might be: A partner who will give them significant time alone every day

Scripture to help balance fears: He shielded him and cared for him; he guarded him as the apple of his eye. Deut32:10NIV

Choleric

If many of the items on your lists match up with the following, your primary influence may be Choleric

Strengths	Weaknesses
strong-willed	sarcastic
inspirational	domineering
fast-paced	inconsiderate
determined	cruel when angry
independent	self-reliant
intuitive	unemotional
personable, outgoing	proud
disciplined, efficient	
task-oriented	
confident leader	

Relationship Notes About Cholerics

They are very strong and opinionated but can be insensitive and uncaring.

On date night a Choleric might often say: "Let's do whatever's practical!"

Qualities you'll love: Charming; inspirational; driven; a high-achieving visionary

Tendencies that might be difficult to deal with in marriage: Tend to dominate every conversation with their viewpoints; hot-tempered; work so hard they often burn out or get ill; unemotional; always right

Highest hurdles: Hardheadedness and self-will

Heart-cry of the Choleric: "Of course I'm right!"

Greatest fear: Being useless, purposeless

Greatest need in marriage might be: A spouse who can be practical, flexible, and even-keeled

Scripture to help balance fears: On the seventh day, having finished his task, God rested from all his work.^{Gen2:2NLT}

Phlegmatic

If many of the items on your lists match up with the following, your primary influence may be Phlegmatic.

Strengths	**Weaknesses**
stable	slow-paced
flexible	self-righteous
calm	stubborn to change
efficient	fearful, worrier
perfectionistic	indecisive
practical	low-energy
peacemaker	self-protective
good sense of humor	unmotivated, uninspired

Relationship Notes About Phlegmatics

They are very easygoing but can be hard to motivate and low on energy.

On date night a Phlegmatic might often say: "Let's do whatever's easiest!"

Qualities you'll love: Always on time; calm, even when expressing anger; flexible

Tendencies that might be difficult to deal with in marriage: Can be cheapskates; sarcastic and stubborn; are often couch potatoes; love naps; do everything slowly and methodically

Highest hurdles: Lack of motivation and procrastination

Heart-cry of the Phlegmatic: "Can't we just get along?"

Greatest fear: A disturbance of their peace

Greatest need in marriage might be: A peaceful home with no arguing

Scripture to help balance fears: You will keep him in perfect peace, whose mind is stayed on You, because he trusts in You.[Isa26:3]

Supine

If many of the items on your lists match up with the following, your primary influence may be Supine.

Strengths	Weaknesses
servant spirit	harbors anger
relationship oriented	indecisive
loves tasks	manipulative
gentle	weak-willed
dependable	lacks initiative
loyal	insecure
diligent	

Relationship Notes About Supines

They love to serve and are outgoing only if they feel liked and "invited in" by others.

On date night a Supine might often say: "Let's do whatever you want to do."

Qualities you'll love: Very self-sacrificing; gentle and humble

Tendencies that might be difficult to deal with in marriage: Tend to be indecisive; send mixed messages; have difficulty with confrontation which causes them to internalize anger and expect you to be a mind reader regarding what's wrong; may always wait for spouse to initiate sex

Highest hurdles: Learning how to express anger and other needs; overcoming a weak will

Heart-cry of the Supine: "Why doesn't anyone appreciate me?"

Greatest fear: That others think they're worthless

Greatest need in marriage might be: A partner who will take the lead in all decision making

Scripture to help balance fears: But you are a chosen generation, a royal priesthood, a holy nation, His own special people.[1Pet2:9]

When you understand each other's temperaments—and are able to communicate about them—you can minimize misunderstandings and surprises as you move forward in your relationship. Bring any significant temperament concerns you found (which can be slow relationship killers!) before your PM, and ask Him for supernatural intervention. The results of this exercise can also be used to identify generational or other besetting sins and help you clean house, using the information in Rule 5.

Now, when you juxtapose your intended mate's temperament next to yours and imagine a life together, do you feel more or less empowered to be all you're called to be? Can that person pull you up if you fall? For instance, an easy-going Phlegmatic may do fine with a dominant, high-achieving Choleric mate, while a Supine might get crushed by their insensitivity. A Melancholy might find the exuberance of a fast-moving Sanguine mate initially exciting, but may constantly long for more intimacy and grow increasingly lonely in the marriage.

Encouraging Word

For my yoke fits perfectly,
and the burden I give you is light. Matt11:30NLT

If dealing with your potential mate's temperament
issues weighs you down, is it from Him?

Fortunately, no temperament is totally incompatible with another. That's because few of us are purely any one temperament but a combination of several. It can still be quite challenging to live with someone vastly different from you, but this blending helps to balance out some of the…uh…stronger traits, and makes us easier people to live with.

"KNOW THE GOAL" EXERCISES

Now that you understand more about how each of you is wired, here are some more exercises to help you learn each other's values and goals. Note, however, that you both should go through the questions in Rule 3 (starting on page 35) before you do these exercises. They are intended to help you think through how compatible your potential mate is with the destiny God has written on your heart.

In order to ensure that you do not influence each other, work through each of these exercises alone, and don't talk to the other about what you have written until both of you have completed the exercise. Then set aside some time to share with each other what you feel God has called you to do with your lives.

- *Fifty-Year Plan.* Build on the vision God gave you about your destiny (Rule 3). Be ambitious and write a plan for the next fifty years of your life. What do you believe God is calling you to do over that span of time? Does your potential mate's temperament suit the things you will have to do to accomplish it? For instance, if you need to get an MBA or a seminary degree in order to achieve the goal God put in your heart, is your potential spouse willing to sacrifice expensive dates in order to help you save toward that end? If God has given you a vision of adopting kids from a foreign country, will your potential mate support that plan? Is he willing to give up golf or premium cable channels so you can save money? Is she willing to buy fewer clothes or give up her weekly manicure for "the cause"?

- *Ten Years Backward.* Break the fifty-year plan down into ten-year increments, and note what needs to be done each decade to achieve that plan. Ask yourself what ingredients will be required in terms of sacrifice, financial commitment, absence from home, social obligations, and so on. Commit to meet with your potential spouse regularly to discuss where both of you see yourselves in ten years. Be candid about what it would involve. Then work backward from the ten-year goal, one year at a time.

We know this is tedious work, but the exercise will prove worthwhile and will unearth many sobering discoveries about yourself and your potential Mr. or Mrs. Right. Don't interject your opinion too much, just facilitate. You will learn a lot about whether you are on the same page.

- *Pizza Pie Priorities.* Ask your potential mate to list his or her spiritual, social, physical, family, ministry, and financial goals in order of priority. Do you see evidence that he or she is actively working on those goals?
- *Living Obituary.* Write down what you hope is said about you at your funeral, in fifty words or less. Then share your thoughts with each other.
- *Value Added.* Identify the top ten values that characterize your life. Cut the list down to seven, then five, then three. Identify which value:
  1. is absolutely essential for your peace of mind;
  2. you could not imagine living without;
  3. would be the one you would take with you to a desert island.

If the exercises in this rule don't help you understand one another better, we don't know what will! Habakkuk 2:2 says we should *write the vision, and make it plain upon tables, that he may run that readeth it.*[KJV] You don't want a spouse who runs away when he or she reads your vision—you want someone who will run alongside you to achieve those things that are exceedingly and abundantly more than you could have asked or thought.[seeEph3:20]

Handle the Heat

Be ye angry, and sin not.

—Ephesians 4:26, KJV

How many horrifying cases of domestic violence have you heard about in the news over the past year? Clearly, anger can be dangerous. Uncontrolled anger has ruined marriages and friendships, left ugly scars on children, and led to many a career casualty. It is probably responsible for more unhappiness in our society than any other issue.

It can be devastating to marry someone, only to discover that he or she has a serious anger problem: He sends verbal missiles your way every time you ask about his job situation, or she gives you the Frappuccino freeze whenever you bring up her father. Few things dishonor a relationship more than angry words or actions in the heat of an argument. And far too many people have unchanneled anger that they finally express in explosive outbursts, usually with the person they are closest to. Others hold all of their anger inside and do harm to themselves. God has a better way.

According to God's Word, it's fine to be angry—it's what we do with that anger that God is most concerned about. "Some people express anger in aggressive ways, which is a symptom of uncontrolled anger," notes psychologist Dr. Rick Holmes. "What's worse is that when we do the aggressive act, bitterness often sets in. Couples must learn to be assertive, not aggressive, in the expression of their anger so they can live out the principle of this passage in their relationship."[6] If we express aggressive anger when we have disagreements in our pre-marriage relationships—when we are on our "best behavior"—we'll do the same or worse in a marital dispute. It's critical to check ourselves and our potential Mr. or Mrs. Right in this area now.

One traditional father decided to test his daughter's boyfriend's anger management skills before the two got engaged. He contacted the man and asked him over for breakfast to talk about his daughter. Time: 6:00 a.m. The boyfriend agreed and showed up promptly, only to sit in the kitchen for twenty minutes because the dad hadn't showered yet. To make a long story short, breakfast had not been made (Mom decided to sleep in), and the father proceeded to pontificate about the perils of marrying ill-advised for the next forty-five minutes without pause. Then he added insult to injury by standing up while the boyfriend was in midsentence (one of the few he got in), extending his hand, and walking off.

What was this dad up to? He was checking to see how his daughter's boyfriend would respond if faced with all four of her weaknesses at once: she liked to get up before dawn; she was often late for appointments; she wasn't too keen on cooking; and she loved to talk. We hope this young man knew how to be *angry and sin not* with his future father-in-law and was not just waiting to take it out on his girlfriend later!

How would your potential Mr. or Mrs. Right do if presented with a similar test? How do *you* handle the heat? Do you know how to *be angry and sin not?* What does the Bible have to say about anger? Let's find out.

No One Makes Us Angry

God's Word says, *I call heaven and earth as witnesses today against you, that I have set before you life and death, blessing and cursing; therefore* **choose** *life, that both you and your descendants may live.*[Deut30:19] In other words, no one and no thing causes you to feel anger, so strike this phrase from your vocabulary: "You make me so angry!" We often get angry because we feel hurt inside, and something or someone on the outside triggered that hurt. Sometimes we just want retribution for a wrong done to us. Whatever the case, the angry response comes from within. We can decide to *respond* to our hurt in a calm, positive manner (assertive), or we can decide to *react* by expressing anger aggressively. The angry outburst itself is a red light on the dashboard, signaling trouble somewhere deeper.

If we are prone to bouts of anger, we need to check under our emotional, spiritual, and relational hoods to identify the root of the problem. Though we may have considerable baggage triggering our angry responses, each of us is ultimately responsible for how we act. Resolve to exercise self-control in situations that trigger ungodly responses to anger and to rule over your own spirit. *He who is slow to anger is better than the mighty, and he who rules his spirit than he who takes a city.*[Prov16:32] *Whoever has no rule over his own spirit is like a city broken down, without walls.*[25:28]

Anyone who has tried to tame his or her temper knows it requires more than three points and a poem. So how can you begin to rule over your spirit? Recognize that the power source for controlling anger is the Holy Spirit. *For God did not give us a spirit of timidity (of cowardice, of craven and cringing and fawning fear), but [He has given us a spirit] of power and of love and of calm and well-balanced mind and discipline and self-control.*[2 Tim 1:7 AMP] We can start the process by asking for our PM's help in identifying and understanding how we handle the heat.

FIGHTING THE FURY STARTS EARLY

We establish a pattern for how to handle anger as children, even as babies. Our parents play a large role in shaping whether we express or implode our angry feelings. Proverbs 15:1 says, *A soft answer turns away wrath, but a harsh word stirs up anger.* If our parents constantly spoke harshly to us, we may have grown up angry. If we have never addressed that anger, it has likely grown larger as we've matured. That's why Ephesians 6:4 commands fathers to *provoke not your children to wrath.*[KJV] Angry children believe the world is an angry place and grow up to be angry adults.

On the other hand, some parents encourage their kids to hush up every angry feeling for "the sake of peace." That was the case for me (Pam). I learned (and had to unlearn as an adult) how to sulk, pout, and refuse to talk for days if I was angry. When I was a teenager I developed a stomach condition, and no medical root could be found for it except stress. It was not until I was older that I realized the stress was due to unexpressed anger—and that if I didn't learn how to handle anger in a godly way, I would do further harm to my body.

What did your family teach you about handling the heat? "Kids learn to lash out when they feel rejected, are teased, or have their feelings belittled," offers Dr. Holmes, who often works with troubled children and adults with anger issues. "When they get older they still react out of habit, replaying an old tape from childhood that needs to be modified or erased."[7] Ask your PM to help you recognize any destructive patterns in your life, remove them, and learn how to manage your anger in a godly way. (We will talk more about how to do this.) What triggers your anger? Common triggers include:

- unmet needs
- the perception that someone is being aggressive toward you
- feeling taken advantage of or victimized
- frustrated expectations when things did not work out the way you thought they would, or people didn't perform the way you expected
- insecurity
- fear of loss
- physical or emotional pain of some kind
- feeling attacked or being dealt with unfairly by someone

The things from the above list that trigger inappropriate anger in you act like a sperm trying to unite with the egg of your vulnerability. To avoid anger's conception, use the birth control of Scripture memorization. If you see yourself on this list, invest in a good study Bible with a topical index, for example, the *Life Application Bible* or the *Thompson Chain Reference Study Bible*. Both offer instant references so you can find scriptures by topic. This will help you develop an arsenal of weapons to use whenever you are tempted to revert to old anger patterns.

Once you've explored how you handle anger and have identified its roots, turn the spotlight on your intended. Talk candidly with your

Mr. or Mrs. Right about how his or her family handles anger. Note
and discuss any destructive patterns. Check to see if you notice any
of the following examples of ungodly expressions of anger in your
intended mate:

- use of profanity
- radical swings in temperament
- overreaction to minor things; easily agitated
- inability to stop discussing or analyzing trivial issues
- victim mind-set ("Everyone's against me.")
- irrational outbursts

Some people who are depressed or who hold all their angry feelings inside feel momentarily euphoric when they lash out—it actually
makes them feel alive. Thus they almost enjoy opportunities to
express anger aggressively, because it gives them a chance to feel something other than depression or suppression. If you see evidence of this
in your intended mate—run. The underlying issues behind this level
of anger must be dealt with at a deep spiritual level—don't allow
yourself to be the punching bag!

Encouraging Word
For His anger is but for a moment,
*His favor is for life.*Ps30:5

When you become angry with someone,
how long does your anger last?

If your potential mate refuses to talk about or get help for his or
her anger problem, give careful thought to what you're getting into.
The negative outcome and life-altering consequences of poorly man-

aged anger are too great to leave to hope! (See more on identifying anger's roots in Rule 5.)

Not only do you need to check out how each of you handles the heat, you also need to understand what the Bible has to say about how we can handle our anger in a godly way, beginning with what not to do.

UNGODLY RESPONSES TO ANGER

King Saul is a great example of the self-destructive nature of unchecked anger. Many people are like him—engulfed with anger, jealousy, and a bevy of negative emotions. Saul was chosen by God to be king, but he basically slept on the job. So God handpicked another king, David. As the anointing faded from Saul and flourished in David, Saul grew green with envy. Even the ladies applauded David. *So the women sang as they danced, and said: "Saul has slain his thousands, and David his ten thousands." Then Saul was very angry, and the saying displeased him.*[1Sam18:7-8]

Saul, or anyone in that situation, could have taken one of two routes. He could have gone to God in his brokenness and humility and cried out his pain. If he was sincere, God would have received him, comforted him, and spoken to him in love about his flaws. His restoration could have been great if he obeyed God's counsel. But he had an in-and-out relationship with God and so didn't seek His advice. Instead, he allowed his fall from fame and his envy of David to ruin him.

Cain offers another example of what happens when our anger remains unchecked. As the firstborn of Adam and Eve, Cain might have been a little cocky. He was a farmer while his brother, Abel, was a shepherd. They both brought sacrifices to God, as was the custom in the Old Testament. Cain brought fruit, and Abel brought fat from the firstborn of his flock.

> And the LORD respected Abel and his offering, but He did not respect Cain and his offering. And Cain was very angry, and his countenance fell.
>
> So the LORD said to Cain, "Why are you angry? And why has your countenance fallen? If you do well, will you not be accepted? And if you do not do well, sin lies at the door. And its desire is for you, but you should rule over it."
>
> Now Cain talked with Abel his brother; and it came to pass, when they were in the field, that Cain rose up against Abel his brother and killed him.[Gen4:4-8]

Like Saul, Cain had two choices. He could have given in to his anger and bitterness, or he could have turned to God with his hurt. Interestingly, God gave Cain a tip. He told him, "If you'll get your heart attitude together, I'll accept your offerings too. And if you take care of your mistake maturely, I know you can overcome the temptation to sin." But Cain chose to interpret the event as a rejection and to act out his pain—and he is now listed in the Biblical Hall of Fame as the world's first murderer.

GODLY RESPONSES TO ANGER

Anger is an emotion that happens in the normal course of life. If Saul and Cain had dealt with their anger in a godly way, they would not have sinned. Anger becomes sin when it degenerates into uncontrolled or inappropriate behavior. This is a very important distinction: God says it's okay to be angry. Just make sure that a lack of self-control does not cause you to engage in behavior that is inconsistent with godliness.

Take a lesson from Nehemiah, an excellent leader in the fourth century BC. He was in charge of a huge construction project in Jerusalem:

Nine Steps to Anger Management

Many of our poor anger-management traits have been practiced and perfected since childhood. Like a glass of warm milk and a blankie, they are comforting to us because they are familiar. It will take prayer, commitment, and repetition in order to turn things around in this area. Here are the steps:

1. *Confess it.* Go to the person and let him or her know how you feel.[see1John1:9]
2. *Trace it.* Find the cause of your anger; be angry at the problem, not the person.[seeJames4:8]
3. *Accept it.* Take personal responsibility.[seeDeut30:19]
4. *Train it.* Hold your tongue until you cool down.[seeGal5:23]
5. *Work it.* Channel your anger in a healthy way.[seeNeh5]
6. *Control it.* Regain self-control by relinquishing control to Christ.[seeGal2:20]
7. *Starve it.* Don't nurse a grudge.[seeMark11:25]
8. *Expose it.* Be open and honest with others about what riles you.[seePs51:6]
9. *Free it.* Set your spirit free by praying for the person who has injured you.[seeJames5:16]

rebuilding the walls and gates of the city. An equal opportunity employer, he hired both the rich and the poor to do the job. But a conflict arose between the two groups, and Nehemiah learned that the poor workers were being exploited by the rich ones. Nehemiah said, *I became very angry when I heard their outcry.*[Neh5:6] In other words, he got righteously angry for a good reason. But he didn't let his anger rage unchecked. Let's look at how he handled his righteous anger, step by step, and note the lessons we can learn from his method.

NEHEMIAH...	LESSON FOR US
• *pondered* the issue	• *Think* before you make a move in anger.
• *spoke out against* those doing wrong	• Use words to *clearly express* the reason for your displeasure.
• *demanded* their accountability and allowed them time to defend themselves	• *Give* the other person *adequate time* to contemplate and rebut or repent.
• *exacted* a fair recompense for the poor, and urged the rich to accept it	• *Seek a solution* to the underlying problem and present it.
• End result: *They agreed to do it*	• *Remember* that your goal is agreement.

At the end of this biblical conflict, everyone, rich and poor, was happy and praising the Lord![seeNeh5] (Lesson: If you can both make up and praise God after an argument, you've done well!)

In Rule 12 you met Abigail, who was married to a fool named Nabal. Not only did Abigail know how to make David feel like a king, she also knew how to dissipate a person's anger. We can do the same. Here's a breakdown of what she did, as relayed in 1 Samuel 25.

When Abigail heard that her husband had ticked off the king she decided to intervene to try to avoid a catastrophe. First, she fed David and his army some good home cooking. (Lesson: Feed a man well before you argue with him…[smile]. Be kind, even when you disagree.) Then she bowed down low before him. (Lesson: A dose of humility often dissipates anger.) She also accepted blame on behalf of Nabal and asked for forgiveness. (Lesson: If you are wrong, admit it.) Then she asked to be heard. (Lesson: Ask if you may explain your side of the story. It shows great respect to the other person.) She reminded David that he was destined for greatness and, as such, should not have a murder on his conscience. (Lesson: Say something nice about the other person, remind him of who he is in Christ, and discourage further arguing.) The Holy Spirit can and will prompt you to do and say the right things, if you'll calm down and listen.

Of course, at times aggressive anger is appropriate and godly. Jesus's godly outburst at the temple demonstrates this truth. He was incensed at some merchants who were swindling people as they entered the temple for worship, and he was so irritated that He overturned their tables.[see Matt 21:12] This is an example of righteous indignation. Jesus's anger was an aggressive response to something that was an abomination to the house of God. This illustrates the fact that there are going to be rare occasions when aggressive responses are necessary. Here's an example: If you came home and found your spouse beating your son to a pulp or sexually molesting your daughter, you would intervene, probably with physical force. And your anger would be a godly response. But if you get enraged when your intended mate is

Living It Out: Paul and Jen's Story

Paul: When Jen and I got serious, I had a high-stress job and got little sleep due to a medical condition, so I handled anger by stuffing it down and avoiding conflict. I thought our issues would work themselves out. I grew up in a home where my dad yelled and screamed a lot and my mom just took it—so I would stuff down my upset feelings and then explode.

Jen: When we began to disagree constantly about our wedding plans, I developed a very harsh way of expressing anger. I thought I had to protect myself from being taken advantage of, so I would yell on top of Paul's voice, and even throw things at him.

Paul: After we got married things just got worse. Jen's anger was very scary, which made me suppress even more. Then I would explode over things that didn't warrant an explosion. God used our external stresses to bring out the buried issues we had inside. Early on, we saw that something was very wrong.

Jen: I grew up in a boarding school with no male authorities. Now here was this guy telling me to be submissive to him. It didn't seem fair. I also thought Paul was more lenient with himself than he was with me. His actions and tone told me he had zero confidence in me. I didn't really trust him or any male figure, so I questioned everything he said or did.

Paul: After we married I never knew when an argument would erupt. I would bring up her childhood as a reason for how Jen handled conflict, and she would rebuff it and yell, "How dare you? I'm over that!" I decided she had her head in the sand and focused the blame on her, which kept me from dealing with myself.

Jen: By this point, I had had enough and was ready to leave Paul. I had no friends or family around, and no understanding of God's power. I would cry all the time and ask Him to be real to me. Slowly, God started changing my attitude toward Him.

Paul: The real change in me came when I joined a men's accountability group. One of the men told me, "God wants to heal you," and "He wants to meet you where you're at." I realized that I served a small God compared

(continued on next page)

to his. I believed in Jesus theoretically, but
when it came to everyday life, I had no God.
This guy had power for living! All at once
I realized that I was a failure and that my
marriage was failing. A little booklet, from
a well-known ministry, called *Following
God's Plan for Your Life* changed my perspective totally. For the first time I had hope
that my marriage could turn around, and
that I could be the husband I was supposed
to be.

Jen: I questioned whether the change in Paul was
permanent. *Would he live it out at home?* I
wondered. I had gone far away from my husband in my heart, which I believe is where
divorce begins. It took me some time to
change that. Though I had accepted Christ,
God was still a concept to me. I had faith,
but there was still a disconnect because
Christ was not the center of my life.

Paul: We began attending a new Bible study
together and learned about God's purpose
for our lives. I realized that God had to work
on me first, so I gobbled up books and
memorized scriptures (instead of the novels
I used to devour weekly). God began to

soften both our hearts. The scriptures I
memorized gave me the ability to take a
few seconds out before reacting to Jen. I
realized that I could no longer keep mentally
replaying our arguments. Instead, I needed
to meditate on those scriptures or pray
for Jen.

Jen: Now I constantly ask the Holy Spirit for
counsel regarding Paul. And He often tells
me to let it go and shut up! Usually, He
brings Paul around. So I don't worry about
how to word things perfectly or how I'm
going to approach something with him. I just
ask the Lord. If I said a hundred stupid things
to my husband before, now I say fifty!

Paul: It's great because now humor takes over in
our disagreements, and there's a lightheart-
edness in our marriage that wasn't there
before. There's peace in our home now
because the Word of God reigns. We're
willing to give each other a lot more room,
compassion, leniency, and grace. We have a
sense that we're not alone, because we
both have put God first. We're His adver-
tisement, so He has a vested interest in our
success!

late for a dinner date or forgets to send you flowers on Valentine's Day, you have an anger-management problem. Aside from abuse and acts of violence, we can think of very few things that your intended mate might do that could biblically warrant a Jesus-and-the-money-changers type of response.

God gets angry with our sinful ways, our perversions, and abuses of one another. But His overall nature is to love us, be patient with us, forgive us, and to be long-suffering, knowing that we can change. He guides us into that change by speaking the truth in love to us, chastising us, and giving us boundaries so we don't hurt ourselves and others. We should determine to do no less with each other.

Fallout from Anger

Perhaps you are saying, "This really doesn't apply to us. Everything else about JohnBoy or CoraLee is so wuuuunderful. I'm sure this anger thing will pass." We caution you to rethink your position. Whenever we compromise the standards God has outlined in His Word, we will experience the fallout. Take note of the toll that poor anger management takes on a relationship.

Prevents Transparency

In order for a relationship to reach peak levels of "into-me-see," there must be honesty, openness, and acceptance. None of these crucial components can be achieved if either person is afraid of arousing anger in the other. If your relationship is characterized by uncontrolled outbursts of anger, you will do a mental computation every time you want to share your feelings. If you decide to keep your feelings to yourself, your dinner conversations will go like this: "So, how was your day?" "Fine." "What'd you do today?" "Nothing unusual." "How's work going?" "Great." "What's wrong?" "Nothing. Why does something have to be wrong?" And so on. This is not the picturesque married life you envisioned!

Leaves Indelible Marks on the Soul

We stated earlier that the reason many people are walking through life angry is because of harsh words spoken to them early in their lives. One of the most tragic phenomena in our country is the number of adults who still bear scars and sores from what Mom or Dad said or did to them as a child. This is a direct result of Satan's work. He is happy when something that was done to you at age four still paralyzes you at age forty, and he knows that harsh words can damage the human spirit. Proverbs 18:14 says, *The spirit of a man will sustain him in sickness, but who can bear a broken spirit?* We can withstand a physical sickness in our body as long as our spirit is not broken—yet angry words break the spirit. So if your intended has angry outbursts, don't shrug it off. Pay attention *to* it now, so you won't suffer *in* it later.

Causes Us to Engage in Conduct We'll Regret

All of us can say we have sometimes conducted ourselves in ways we regret. It might have been words or actions, but at times we fail to exercise one of the most precious fruits of the Spirit: self-control. While some anger-management gurus promote a strategy that says to "just hit something; you'll feel better," according to Dr. Holmes and other experts, this is bad advice. "The idea that you should just get your anger out in any way, shape or form, is damaging," he adds.

"Whatever physical action you take doesn't deal with the underlying issue that triggered the anger. It's still there."[8] Often the real solution lies in destroying the wrong beliefs embedded in a person early in life.

People who release anger in aggressive ways are also often the "last hired and first fired." Their interpersonal skills suffer because no one wants to tangle with them, in the office or at home. They become isolated and alienated. Unresolved anger always matures into bitterness, and people do heinous things when under that yoke. That is why it's so important to deal with anger constructively.

Affects Our Health and Can Shorten Our Lives

Few people realize the negative influence that constant fits of anger can have on your health. It causes your emotions to run amuck and can send your blood pressure sky high, increasing your susceptibility to a myriad of other illnesses. Several studies reported in *The Journal of the American Medical Association* (JAMA) bear out the relationship between anger, marital stress, deteriorating health, and even death:

- Acute life stressors, including episodes of extreme anger, were shown to trigger myocardial infarction (heart attack) and premature death in men. Interestingly, angry episodes were put in the same category of "acute stressors" as were earthquakes and terrorist attacks![9]

- An unhappy marriage was shown to be an important life stressor, and divorced men have been shown to have higher mortality rates than married men.[10]

- Hostility was found to be the behavioral trait most reliably associated with increased incidence of hypertension and coronary heart disease.[11]

- And just the title of this JAMA study says it all: "Marital Stress Worsens Prognosis in Women with Coronary Heart Disease."[12]

If bouts of anger increase marital stress, and stress increases our risk of developing everything from migraine headaches to heart attacks to stroke to depressed immune systems, we'd be wise to address the root problem.

Hurts Our Testimony and Witness

People are turned off for the long haul when they observe Christians who lack self-control and burst into fits of anger. Before we can win people to faith in Christ, we must win them to ourselves. And let's face it, who would be interested in our faith if our conduct outside of church is repugnant? This leaves people saying, "Why would I want to serve a God like *that*?"

As Christians, we should be the last ones characterized as angry people. In fact, the quality that should set us apart from the pack is our ability to forgive, just as we were forgiven by God—and continue to be on a daily basis! *Selah.*

THE ULTIMATE ANTACID

Forgiveness is the oil that keeps relationships running. It is not an event but a lifestyle. Make it a conscious, everyday practice now—especially after disagreements—and you'll do your marriage well. There is nothing more Christlike than to forgive a person when he or she least deserves it.

Again, it is inevitable that you'll become offended in relationships—even Jesus said so:

It is impossible that no offenses should come, but woe to him through whom they do come! It would be better for him if a mill- stone were hung around his neck, and he were thrown into the sea, than that he should offend one of these little ones. Take heed to yourselves. If your brother sins against you, rebuke him; and if he repents, forgive him. And if he sins against you seven times in a day, and seven times in a day returns to you, saying, "I repent," you shall forgive him. [Luke17:1-4]

How did the apostles respond to this grand command? Basically, they said, "Help us, Lawd Jesus!" They said to Him: *Increase our faith.*[v5] Boy, do these words echo in our soul when we want to choke the person we are in a relationship with and cuss him or her all the way down Main Street (lovingly, of course)!

It takes faith to forgive someone and to trust God to handle these situations. We must develop the mind-set that forgiveness is a com- mand. It is our responsibility before a mighty God. *Forgive us our sins, just as we have forgiven those who have sinned against us.*[Matt6:12NLT]

We can choose to cultivate one of two environments in our rela- tionships: the Acid or the Antacid. Ephesians 4 describes these two opposing environments, beginning with the acidic: *Let all bitterness, wrath, anger, clamor, and evil speaking be put away from you, with all malice.*[v31] Here's a quick exegesis of these five acids:

- *Bitterness*—an irritable, angry, and critical state of mind. *Satan's hope:* this internal attitude will take over your counte- nance and destroy you from within.
- *Anger and wrath*—temper; and a strong, vengeful expression of anger, respectively. *Satan's hope:* to have any marital dispute

escalate to where the exchange leaves indelible scars, making reconciliation seem impossible.

- *Clamor*—loud yelling. *Satan's hope:* to get you to focus so much on out-screaming each other that you'll move far away from the point of the discussion and never reach reconciliation.
- *Evil speaking*—to slander or malign another person. *Satan's hope:* you heap up offenses with every slanderous word you speak; that you'll gossip and feel guilty at the communion table.^see1Cor11:27-30
- *Malice*—the intent to do harm, even physically. *Satan's hope:* as you allow bitterness to get its full expression, you will commit a heinous crime and perhaps kill yourself afterward.

The next verse describes the Antacid environment, characterized by forgiveness. *And be kind to one another, tenderhearted, forgiving one another, even as God in Christ forgave you.*^Eph4:32 Think of forgiveness as the milk of magnesia that keeps a relationship in balance. Here's an exegesis of these three "warm milk" words:

- *Kind*—useful, virtuous, good, mild, pleasant, benevolent (as opposed to harsh, hard, sharp, or bitter)
- *Tenderhearted*—compassionate, easily moved to love, pity, or sorrow
- *Forgiving*—to do something pleasant or agreeable, to pardon, to graciously restore one to another, to do a favor to, to gratify, to show one's self gracious, kind, benevolent, to give freely, to bestow

In the words of Joshua, *choose for yourselves this day* what type of atmosphere you both will allow to reign in your relationship.^24:15

Know that if you don't actively decide to cultivate the Antacid environment in your relationship *now*, you will passively accept the Acid trip.

Life is too short to have a relationship consumed with inappro-

How to Break Up in Three Easy Steps

We are, of course, kidding with this title—breaking up is *not* easy. But we think every man and woman should learn how to end a relationship if they find they have irresolvable differences, without devastating the other person. If you have a habit of ending a relationship by a sudden disappearance, an angry explosion, or by just "letting things fizzle out," your actions just add insult to injury. We don't think that's God-honoring, so we offer these three steps. Let your PM, the Holy Spirit, show you what to say in your particular situation.

1. *Act immediately.* Few things are as unfair as leading a person down a garden path, allowing him or her to think a relationship is moving forward when it's not. Life is too short not to act promptly when you know that a relationship has no future.

2. *Speak the truth in love.*^seeEph4:15 This is key to breaking up well. Too many unhealthy relationships linger on, because one and sometimes both participants fail to tell the truth in a loving way. The Enemy wants us to ignore the warning signals of our PM and keep us entrapped in unhealthy relationships way too long. Psalm 51:6 tells us that God desires truth in our

priate expressions of anger. Why engage in something that makes you deteriorate emotionally, mentally, physically, and spiritually? Count the cost lest you become another notch on Satan's belt of angry Christian casualties.

> inward being. What a powerful statement. Are we submitting to the truth regarding the direction of this relationship if we know that something "ain't happenin'"? If peace is your umpire and you no longer have peace about the time you are spending with someone in courtship, you must stop wasting the other person's time—and your own.
>
> 3. *Seek to edify the person if possible.* If you have decided to terminate a relationship because of incompatibilities or because of something lacking in the other person's character, we implore you to take the high road and point out all of the positive things you experienced in your time with the person. If the relationship became unpleasant, still try to edify the other person. Be respectful. You might say, "Your conduct has been very disturbing to me. While I don't believe it is representative of the best in you, I can't allow you to hurt me any longer. I forgive you and believe God will continue to minister to you and reveal how you can express your better qualities." In addition, admit your own faults that contributed to the demise of the relationship.

Listen More, Talk Less

Let every man be swift to hear, slow to speak.

—JAMES 1:19

Shouldn't the above verse read: *Let every man be swift to hear and every woman be slow to speak?* Okay, we won't rewrite the Bible, but we want to acknowledge that most communication problems in relationships stem from the desire to be heard rather than to listen—and both genders are equally guilty. Conflicts arise because two self-centered individuals are trying to get their points across at the same time. While one person is talking, the other is either busily formulating his or her comeback/quick solution/next long-winded story, or worse, reaching for the remote control. Neither is listening to the other; neither is focusing on the other. No one feels heard or understood. (And date night ends early.)

We practice these poor communication skills in our relationship with God too. We blurt out a list of requests, pleas, and problems to Him—and then we're off to the rest of our day. Often, we come up with bright solutions to our problem without even asking Him to chime in. When was the last time you just sat quietly in the presence of God for more than a minute and waited for Him to speak? I (Pam) know that I don't do this often enough. The Lord has to resort to speaking to me softly when my brain and my tongue are on pause—

usually in the shower, washing dishes, or just before I fell asleep. When I'm more relaxed, I'm able to give Him my full attention and can hear Him better.

The message of this rule is simple: If we're always too distracted to listen or too busy flapping our gums, we'll miss the voice of the Holy Spirit (who always wants to weigh in on our choice of a mate), and we'll set ourselves up for poor communication in marriage.

The ready listener, as described in James 1:19, makes a conscious decision to have healthy communication. The word *communicate* comes from a root word meaning "to hold in common." To truly communicate means that you take what is in your heart and place it in another person's heart, and he or she does the same with you. So when you speak, you are giving away important pieces of yourself; and when you listen, you are receiving what's in the other person's heart. (And you didn't think talking was romantic!)

COMMUNICATION MEETS A DEEP NEED IN US

Philippians 2:3-4 says, *Let nothing be done through selfish ambition or conceit, but in lowliness of mind let each esteem others better than himself. Let each of you look out not only for his own interests, but also for the interests of others.* As we've said, for a relationship to be successful the needs of both people must be met. To do this, each partner must think about the other person's interests before his or her own. What does this have to do with communication? Everything.

When God the Father sent us Jesus, He communicated His deep love for us by meeting our need for spiritual connection. By creating Eve, God met the need in Adam for a mate—one Adam did not even know he had. God was looking out for our interests and anticipating our needs, communicating how much He cared for us.

Most of us desire to be in a relationship with someone who understands our deepest emotions of joy, fear, and excitement—someone who really "gets" us. Sadly, this is hard to find, even in marriage. The problem seems more acute for women than for men. In one population-based study, about 90 percent of women surveyed said they were their spouse's closest confidant, but only 75 percent said that their mate was theirs. Most women also named a relative, usually another female, as their primary source of social support, where men named their wives as this source much more often.[13] Ponder the huge number of people who spend more than a hundred dollars an hour just to have someone listen to them—either on a counselor's couch, on a barstool, or in a seedy hotel room.

Unmet emotional needs are one of the biggest causes of divorce. Don't let this happen to you! Learn to become a good listener and a slow speaker now, before you get married. This will help you discover two things early: what your potential mate's emotional needs are and how you can meet those needs.

MISTAKES MOST MEN MAKE

Many men acknowledge there are few things more satisfying than having someone give them an empathetic ear when they are facing challenges. But they struggle to give this gift to the women in their lives. A woman gets frustrated when she pours her soul out to a man and he constantly interrupts her with solutions or brings up something completely unrelated to what she's talking about. When women realize that a man is not really listening, they leave the conversation feeling exasperated, sad, angry, or disillusioned about the relationship.

A man cannot understand the nuances a woman is trying to communicate unless he is paying close attention to what she's saying and *how* she is saying it. You can read a lot in a person's tone, facial expression, and body language, but only if you're looking. The message to husbands-to-be is this: The act of hearing tells you there's music playing; the decision to listen gives you the words to the song.

For all of us multitasking listeners, to follow are a few good tips. *The Ready Listener...*

- establishes an environment that is conducive to listening by eliminating distractions (like the television or cell phone);
- seeks to understand what is being communicated before seeking to be understood;
- gives others the opportunity to express their viewpoint without interrupting;
- looks at others in the eye while they are speaking and takes note of their facial expression;
- avoids antagonistic body language (folded arms, back to the person, frowning);
- allows others to finish making their main points and then *asks* if it's okay to respond;
- repeats back what he or she understood without using the opportunity to interject a point;
- guards against unhealthy responses that steal and destroy transparency.

Men certainly aren't the only ones who need to learn to improve their communication skills. To follow are some things women need to focus on.

Mistakes Most Women Make

Women can sometimes vent to their boyfriends in such a dramatic, emotion-packed manner that their men become desensitized to what's really important and what's not. This is particularly true if the drama is routine. A wise wife-in-training keeps in mind that women communicate for *rapport*, while men communicate for *report*. She will be conservative when talking about the mundane (just the facts, ma'am) and thus allow a man to be appropriately attentive when she has something pressing to tell him. Talking too much about small things reveals an element of selfishness and shows a lack of respect for the other person's wiring, time, and opinion. Those of us reared in a two-parent home may have only talked with Dad about the big issues in our lives. (You remember, "Go tell your father!") There was a reason for that! Dad probably wasn't wired to hear every jot and tittle of the back story, the way Mom might have been.

Encouraging Word

*He who answers a matter before he hears it,
it is folly and shame to him.* Prov18:13

What was the last important issue your potential mate discussed with you? Based on what you have read so far in this chapter, were you a ready listener? a slow speaker? Ask your intended mate what he or she thought.

Again, we can learn something about men, women, and communication from the Genesis 2 story of creation. Here we see that Adam was first given a task—to tend the garden and name the animals. He lived a bachelor lifestyle. Eve was first given a relationship—to be a helper to Adam. She never got to be a bachelorette. Adam didn't have to talk to anyone in order to complete his job, but Eve certainly did. Could this be why women tend to want to talk, and men tend to want to work?

For all of us fast talkers, to follow here's some good advice. *The Slow Speaker...*

- is sensitive not to data-dump on others indiscriminately;
- stays open to hearing the truth, even if it goes against what he or she wants to hear;
- avoids retelling an old story in detail if it isn't germane to the issue being discussed;
- makes an effort to speak clearly, calmly, and concisely;
- recognizes the importance of timing when talking about certain topics;
- doesn't press for a response before the other person has had a chance to digest and process what was said;
- shows appreciation for feedback with nonverbal signals (rather than interruptions);
- views conversations as sacred communication and thus is mindful of maintaining the above boundaries.

KEEP THE EARS OF YOUR SPIRIT OPEN

While you are practicing good listening with your potential Mr. or Mrs. Right, it's also important to listen to what your PM is telling you about that person. In the parable of the sower, Jesus ends with this: *To those who are **open** to my teaching, more understanding will be* *given.*^{Mark4:25NLT} So the million-dollar question is this: Are you open to what the Spirit might be trying to say about whether this relationship should move forward? Or are you simply interested in telling Him what you've already decided?

As we've said before, when it comes to the important decision of whom to marry, the Holy Spirit *always* has an opinion. He wants to show you things about your potential mate that you might not see or know. He wants you to have all the information you need to make a wise decision. When you do hear Him speak, it's crucial you allow what you hear to *sink down into your ears.*^{Luke9:44}

Jesus told the disciples to listen like this when He was talking to them about His impending crucifixion. He wanted them to hear well so they could understand the immensity of what was about to happen! He wanted them to understand what He said *in their inner man,* not just in their brains. The same is true about how we hear what the Holy Spirit is telling us about the person we are dating.

This is a great time to go back to Rule 11 and revisit the questions on pages 160-163 in the "Hearing Aids" section (especially if your relationship has progressed since you've been reading this book). Remember, your PM is your Counselor, your Helper, and your Advocate. He is *for* you, so anything He tells you is with your absolute best interests in mind. In the latter stages of courtship, as always, your PM wants to...

- remind you of things He has taught you;^{seeJohn14:26}
- lead and guide you;^{see16:13}
- exhort you to use peace as your umpire.^{seeCol3:15}

If you are in a serious courting or dating relationship, we sincerely hope it is with another mature Christian who believes what you believe. Realize that two people can hold the same general values yet still be widely divergent in their beliefs. Values are general, while beliefs are specific. People can say they value human life but still believe in abortion. The person you are dating or courting may value Christian principles, but that doesn't mean his or her belief system matches yours. For example, I (Pam) dated and almost married a man who valued our Christian faith but firmly believed that the commitment ended with the Sunday church service. As one who enjoyed attending a midweek Bible study and other church fellowship and ministry events, I knew in my heart this wasn't God's best match for me—Christian or not.

If you aren't a ready listener, you are more likely to think the person you are dating believes what you believe when he or she only values what you value. (Get it?) Don't wait until the engagement party to find yourself saying, nervously, "Wow, I never knew you felt *that* way!" Listen now, and discover what things he or she deems important so you will know whether you are heading in the same direction in life. If you neglect this step, you may end up in a lonely and challenging marriage.

If we are serious about growing in the things of God, as evidenced by our choice to attend a good church and weekly Bible study or fellowship and to engage in daily prayer and worship (and reading this book!), our "belief-ability" should be radically expanding. We will hear the advice of our PM and be able to discern those things that are inconsistent with the belief system God has established in us. We'll also be more willing to move along if He says to, even when it hurts. Don't lose the benefit of His guidance in this crucial hour by tuning Him out!

Is That You, God?

Another reason it's important to listen to your potential Mr. or Mrs. Right is that God may want to speak to you *through* that person. This takes real listening, folks. But many Christians don't even try. Why? Pride. Here's an example: A pastor may "close up his spirit" when his wife (who doesn't have a seminary degree, a Bible college diploma, or the call from God to preach) brings up a valid spiritual issue that touches a nerve. He may tell himself, "Oh, she's trying to tell me what to do, to control me." On the other hand, his wife may pull back because she doesn't like his approach or the words he uses. Perhaps she knows too much about him, so she filters his comments or advice through the screen of his last sinful act. Pride can be a major stumbling block to hearing from God through your mate.

God wants us to be able to hear and pick up the nuggets of what He may be trying to say to us through our significant other. If we'll make the effort to listen, we will hear Him speaking through our potential mate. Usually when God speaks to us through another person, we won't "get it" until later when He reinforces it. But if you weren't listening in the first place, you'll miss it. God will often use the person closest to you to reveal things about yourself. Do you have an ear for it? Or do you dismiss it before the sentence even comes out?

Now, not everything our potential mate has to say will be "on point," accurate, or from the throne. Some things won't even be worth listening to. But the *person* is worth listening to and can be used by God to help us grow. He might want to use your potential mate to show you what *not* to do or how *not* to act in certain situations.

This will also alert you to the fact that your mate needs prayer in a certain area (so you can't get proud even when you're "right").

The Bottom Line

Don't settle for a relationship that looks like an old episode of *Married with Children*. You can't really become intimate with someone unless you communicate effectively with him or her, and you can't communicate effectively if you're not willing to listen to that person's character, interests, and heart.

God used sixty-six love letters and more than thirty different authors to make sure He communicated well with us—that's how important He thought it was that we "get Him." The Bible is called the Word of God, not the Thought of God. A word is something that's alive, something you hear, interact with, and can understand.

Hearing is for our own sake; listening is for the sake of the other. If each half of a godly couple practices this, you'll both win.

Tour the High Road

Arise, walk in the land through its length
and its width, for I give it to you.

—GENESIS 13:17

We pray that by reading *His Rules* you've learned the relationship principles that our heavenly Father has laid out clearly in His Word and that you will apply them. When followed, these rules *will* work.

But when you finally get down that aisle, your work is far from over. You cannot afford to kick back and say, "I know it all now; I can relax." So this conclusion will not be an "it is finished" chapter—we must leave you with a charge! Believe it or not, marriage is much easier to *obtain* than to *maintain*. Staying married requires constant upkeep. This should be no surprise, as this principle is true about many other things in our life. You have to change the oil and filters in your car, have periodic tune-ups, and do regularly scheduled maintenance checks. If you don't, your ride will eventually break down, and if it's even worth fixing, the repair bill will be painful.

Yet many people enter marriage thinking it should be like a Jiffy Lube. We shrug off small misunderstandings and miscommunications with our spouse because we need to catch that TV show, run to the gym, work late, or because we just don't want to deal with it. But small problems eventually grow into BIG PROBLEMS. When we don't address them, one or both spouses can develop a root of bitterness that erodes trust and respect and threatens the marriage. *See to it that no one misses the grace of God and that no bitter root grows up to cause trouble and defile many.*^{Heb12:15NIV} If you make this verse your credo before you are engaged or married, you will be better prepared to maintain your future marriage relationship.

We can't say it enough: Just as God must be your primary spouse while you're single, your intimacy with Him must continue into marriage. Make sure you have the following tools in your marriage toolbox, and take heed of the sage principles that keep one fifty-year marriage thriving still. Charge on!

Marriage Maintenance Tools

Keep Your Expectations Realistic

Many married people walk around under a dark cloud saying, "I never seem to do anything that pleases my spouse. I'm never enough." Often the problem isn't them—it's their spouse's unreasonable expectations. One of the fastest ways to suck the life out of your marriage is to place unfair and unattainable demands on your spouse, and then punish him or her for failing to make you happy. Certain areas in our lives can only be refreshed by living water straight from *Him.* By now, you should know what they are. Give your spouse-to-be a wonderful gift—let him or her off the hook for not being God.

Forgive

We've said it before, but it bears repeating: It is inevitable that your spouse will offend you. Make forgiving a conscious, everyday practice in your relationship…beginning today.

Fight a Good Fight

No, we are not encouraging you to institute "fight night" in your home, but rather to fight for the sanctity of your marriage. The apostle Paul said, *I have fought the good fight, I have finished the race, I have kept the faith.*[2Tim4:7] Will you...

- fight the temptation to have an affair or to succumb to competing affections of any kind?
- fight to keep deception out of your marriage?
- fight the temptation to take your spouse for granted?

Be Optimistic

This is the ability to press forward with hope, even when things look bad. We are told that without faith it is impossible to please God.[seeHeb11:6] God wants us to exercise our belief in things that are promised but are not yet apparent. Can you trust Him to bring about desired changes in your marriage? Will you continue to praise God and thank Him for your wife when she's getting on your last nerve? Can you persist in honoring and respecting your husband when he's being less than kingly? Will you listen to the still small voice of your PM, the Holy Spirit, telling you that this time of miscommunication will pass and that soon harmony will return?

Romans 5:8 reminds us that God demonstrates His own love toward us, in that *while we were still sinners, Christ died for us.* Without the guarantee that anybody would accept this wonderful invitation, God still took the risk of giving us His only Son as atonement for our sins. Create and commit to the picture you hold in your heart of what your marriage can be with God's help.

For we walk by faith, not by sight.[2Cor5:7]

Decide to Be Unselfish

If you've ever been around couples made up of two self-centered individuals, you know it's ugly. A married couple is supposed to submit to each other in the fear of God.[seeEph5:21] Get afraid to sin in this area! The word *submit* comes from "sub" and "mission." We are to get under the mission of a Christ-centered marriage, in reverence to God. When a husband loves his wife as Christ loved the church, and a wife is submitting to her husband as unto the Lord, their marriage will flourish. These are the couples we love to be around!

Pursue Mutual Interests

Many couples have separate weekend worlds in which their spouse has no place or is not wanted. In Rule 13, "Watch the Wiring," we learned that we cannot expect to walk together if we're not agreed.[seeAmos3:3] Without mutual interests a couple will look forward to spending their precious little recreation time doing an activity that does not include the other. This sets the relationship up for individualism, loneliness, jealousy, and resentment.

Don't spend your free time pursuing separate interests. Make sure you spend more recreation time together than you do apart. *Two are better than one.*[Eccl4:9]

Keep a Sense of Humor

A sense of humor is crucial to diffuse the tension in a marriage. Someone once said that laughter is the shortest distance between two people. Proverbs 15:13 says, *A cheerful heart brings a smile to your face; a sad heart makes it hard to get through the day.*[MSG]

So whoop it up together every chance you get!

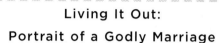

Living It Out:
Portrait of a Godly Marriage

I (Chris) recently went to my parents' home in Atlanta for Mother's Day. My mother had just undergone surgery and was experiencing intense pain, so I couldn't wait to get there and provide her with some moral support and a much-needed hug.

After my father picked me up from the airport, we grabbed a bite to eat. As he proceeded to update me on how my mother was doing, I was amazed at the degree of detail and concern my father expressed. I sat there in total gratitude to the Lord that my parents had each other to grow old together with.

When we arrived home, I walked into their bedroom and hugged my mom. We exchanged welcomes and all of a sudden she turned to me and said, smiling, "I have a new name for your father." I asked, "What is it?" "Mr. Wonderful," she responded. I thought to myself, *Wow! After almost fifty-one years of marriage they are still coming up with new names to extol each other!*

Those words kept echoing in my heart: *Mr. Wonderful.* How did she get to the point in life where she rose above the criticism, stored-up resentment, belittling remarks, and judgmental statements that characterize many marriages, even Christian ones? How could my dad express as much tenderness and concern over the well-being of his wife as

(continued on next page)

he did when they were newlyweds? How had my parents managed to retain the kindle of their romance despite the routines, kids, and all the other challenges of life?

I began to reflect on my lifelong observations of their marriage to get the answers to these questions (and share them with you).

The first thing I recalled was that my parents were always each other's best friends. I have watched them do just about everything together my whole life! They rarely make decisions without consulting each other. They came to the revelation that they were "one flesh" very early on, and as a result of this understanding they have rarely shown each other disrespect. They understand that when you are "one flesh," to hurt the other person is to hurt yourself, and to edify the other person is to edify yourself. Their strongest trait is simply the bond of unity.

My parents constantly affirm each other. Every day while I was growing up they would say things like, "Isn't your mom pretty?" or "Your dad is such a good man!" or "You boys are lucky to have him as a father/her as your mother." These expressions were the norm, not the exception, and as a result peace resided in every room of our house. To this day, people who come to my parents' home are awestruck at the almost tangible presence of the Holy Spirit.

This shouldn't surprise me because my parents taught us the value of prayer from an early age. I've always seen my mother get out of her bed in the morning and drop to her knees to pray before she started her day. Prayer was a staple in our home. This was where I learned that prayer not only starts our day but keeps the family unit together, despite the imperfections we may exhibit from time to time.

Worship is also a major part of their life. If you spend any amount of time with my parents, it won't be long before you hear my father or mother unashamedly belt out a loud "Praise the Lord!" or "God is good!" What always inspires me is that their statements are always so genuine. To them, worship is a lifestyle.

So is forgiveness. My parents are quick to apologize and forgive each other, their three sons, and any other family or friends outside the home. I've always been amazed at their ability to allow offenses to slide off them like water off a duck's back! Even when I tried to "bait" them to seek retribution toward people who had done them "dirty," they categorically refused and quickly reminded me of Christ's commandments to forgive one another so that we also may be forgiven.

As I was flying back home from my Mother's Day visit, it dawned on me that the original manuscript for *His Rules* was written by my parents not on paper but on the heart of anyone who has observed their marriage. They have used respect, encouraging words, prayer, worship, teamwork, and forgiveness to give the world a tangible representation of the harmony and submission that the intangible Trinity displays in heaven.

Commit to Stay the Course

The world is full of people who start out in a blaze of glory but don't make it across the finish line—and so is the Bible. Moses, David, and Solomon all started well but finished poorly. Each did great things for God, but all fell short of what God had called them to be. David in particular illustrates the fact that no amount of public success can make up for being a failure within your own marriage and family.

Can you stay the course when the Enemy is whispering, "Things will never change"? when your family and friends are saying, "If I were you I'd leave"? when you do not feel "in love" no mo'? when medical reports say your spouse has cancer? If you can withstand these types of challenges, then you won't just finish the marriage course; you'll finish with class, honor, and dignity.

Let's commit to following Jesus's example so we, too, are able to say, *I have glorified You on the earth. I have finished the work which You have given Me to do.*John17:4

Use these tools liberally, and you'll place a hedge of protection around your marriage that will be difficult to penetrate. The steady maintenance of your vertical relationship with God will be the biggest factor in the success of your horizontal relationship with your own Mr. or Mrs. Wonderful. Seek after God and His righteousness, and rest assured, a successful marriage will be added unto you.

FINAL RULES FOR THE ROAD

These hard times are small potatoes compared
to the coming good times, the lavish celebration prepared for us.
There's far more here than meets the eye.

The things we see now are here today, gone tomorrow.
But the things we can't see now will last forever.

2 Corinthians 4:17-18, MSG

Keep your eyes on Jesus, who both began and finished this race we're in.
Study how he did it. Because he never lost sight of where he was
headed—that exhilarating finish in and with God—he could put up
with anything along the way: cross, shame, whatever.
And now he's there, in the place of honor, right alongside God.

Hebrews 12:2, MSG

NOTES

Phase One: Get Dieseled

1. Henry Blackaby, *Experiencing God* (Nashville: LifeWay, 1980), 39-40.
2. James Strong, *Strong's Concordance* (Grand Rapids: Zondervan, 2001), s.v. "apokalupsis."
3. A. A. Milne and B. Sibley, *The House at Pooh Corner,* quoted in *The Pooh Book of Quotations* (New York: Dutton, 1991), 63.
4. A. W. Tozer, *The Pursuit of God* (Camp Hill, PA: Christian Publications), 17.
5. John and Paula Sandford, *The Transformation of the Inner Man* (Tulsa, OK: Victory, 1982), 242.
6. Strong, *Concordance,* s.v. "dabaq."
7. Sandford, *Transformation,* 199.

Phase Two: Get Smart

1. Stephen Arterburn and Fred Stoeker, *Every Man's Battle* (Colorado Springs: WaterBrook, 2000), 18.
2. Laurie Hall, *An Affair of the Mind* (Colorado Springs: Focus on the Family, 1996), 65.
3. Michelle McKinney Hammond and Joel A. Brooks Jr., *The Unspoken Rules of Love* (Colorado Springs: WaterBrook, 2003), 86.
4. Strong, *Concordance,* s.v. "teknon" and "huios."
5. Strong, *Concordance,* s.v. "qavah."

6. John C. Maxwell, *The 21 Most Powerful Minutes in a Leader's Day* (Nashville: Nelson, 2000), 43.

7. Strong, *Concordance,* s.v. "teleios."

8. Derek Prince with Ruth Prince, *God Is a Matchmaker* (Grand Rapids: Chosen, 1986), 37-43.

Phase Three: Get Together

1. Materials are from pages 107-122, "Understanding Love," by Dr. Myles Munroe, copyright 2002, used by permission of Destiny Image Publishers, 167 Walnut Bottom Road, Shippensburg, Pennsylvania, 17257, www.destiny image.com.

2. Willard F. Harley Jr., *His Needs, Her Needs: Building an Affair-Proof Marriage* (Grand Rapids: Revell, 1997), jacket flap.

3. They are explicitly told to respect them, but loving them is only implied.[see 1 Pet 3:1-2]

4. Dr. Neil Clark Warren, interview by Joyce Meyer, *Enjoying Everyday Life,* 3-4 February 2004, and reprinted in *Enjoying Everyday Life* (February 2004): 26.

5. Richard and Phyllis Arno, *Creation Therapy: A Biblically-Based Model for Christian Counseling* (Richard and Phyllis Arno, 1993), 1, 5.

6. Holmes, interview.

7. Holmes, interview.

8. Holmes, interview.

9. Karen A. Matthews and Brooks B. Gump, "Chronic Work Stress and Marital Dissolution Increase Risk of Posttrial Mortality in Men from the Multiple Risk Factor

Intervention Trial," *The Journal of the American Medical Association* (JAMA) (February 2002): 309, www.jama.com.

10. Matthews and Gump, "Chronic Work Stress," 309.

11. Lijing L. Yan, Kiang Liu, and others, "Psychosocial Factors and Risk of Hypertension," JAMA (October 2003): 2145, www.jama.com.

12. Kristina Orth-Gomér, Sarah P. Wamala and others, "Marital Stress Worsens Prognosis in Women with Coronary Heart Disease," JAMA (December 2000): 3008-14, www.jama.com.

13. Gomér, Wamala, and others, "Marital Stress Worsens," 3012.

RECOMMENDED READING

On Christian Counseling and Temperament Analysis Profile
Visit the New York Christian Counseling Center Web site
at www.nyccc.org.

On Developing Intimacy with God and a Deeper Prayer Life
Bynum, Juanita. *Matters of the Heart*. Lake Mary, FL:
Charisma, 2002.

Curtis, Brent and John Eldredge. *The Sacred Romance:
Drawing Closer to the Heart of God*. Nashville: Nelson,
1997.

Gire, Ken. *Intimate Moments with the Savior: Learning to
Love*. Grand Rapids: Zondervan, 1989.

Ortlund, Anne. *Disciplines of the Beautiful Woman*. Waco,
TX: Word, 1984.

Sheets, Dutch. *Intercessory Prayer: How God Can Use Your
Prayers to Move Heaven and Earth*. Ventura, CA: Regal,
1996.

Towns, Elmer L. *Fasting for Spiritual Breakthrough*. Grand
Rapids: Zondervan, 1996.

On Discovering Your Destiny and Maximizing Your Potential
Blackaby, Henry. *Experiencing God: Knowing and Doing the Will
of God*. Nashville: LifeWay, 1990.

Covey, Stephen. *The 7 Habits of Highly Effective People*. New
York: Simon & Schuster, 1989.

Maxwell, John C. *The Winning Attitude: Your Key to Personal Success.* Nashville: Nelson, 1993.

Murdock, Mike. *The Assignment.* Tulsa, OK: Albury, 1997.

On Healing the Damaged Soul

McClurkin, Donnie. *Eternal Victim/Eternal Victor.* Lanham, MD: Pneuma Life, 2001.

Omartian, Stormie. *Lord, I Want to Be Whole.* Nashville: Nelson, 2001.

Prince, Derek. *God's Remedy for Rejection.* New Kensington, PA: Whitaker, 1993.

Sandford, John and Paula. *Transformation of the Inner Man.* Tulsa, OK: Victory, 1982.

On Preparation for Marriage

Dobson, James. *Love Must Be Tough/Straight Talk.* Nashville: Word, 1996.

Elliot, Elisabeth. *Passion and Purity: Learning to Bring Your Love Life Under Christ's Control.* Grand Rapids: Revell, 1999.

Prince, Derek and Ruth. *God Is a Matchmaker.* Grand Rapids: Chosen, 1992.

Wilson, P. Bunny. *Knight in Shining Armor.* Eugene, OR: Harvest House, 1995.

———. *Liberated Through Submission.* Eugene, OR: Harvest House, 1990.

On Understanding Men and Women

Arterburn, Stephen, and Dr. Meg J. Rinck, *Avoiding Mr. Wrong.* Nashville: Nelson, 2000.

———. *Finding Mr. Right.* Nashville: Nelson, 2001.

Chapman, Gary. *The Five Love Languages: How to Express Heartfelt Commitment to Your Mate.* Chicago: Northfield, 1992.

Hammond, Michelle McKinney, and Joel A. Brooks Jr. *The Unspoken Rules of Love.* Colorado Springs: WaterBrook, 2003.

Harley, Willard. *His Needs, Her Needs: Building an Affair-Proof Marriage.* Grand Rapids: Revell, 1997.

Huggett, Joyce. *Dating, Sex & Friendship.* Downers Grove, IL: InterVarsity, 1985.

LaHaye, Tim. *Understanding the Male Temperament.* Grand Rapids: Revell, 1977.

Munroe, Myles. *Understanding the Purpose and Power of Men.* New Kensington, PA: Whitaker, 2001.

On Waiting

Goodman, Karon Phillips. *You're Late Again, Lord! The Impatient Woman's Guide to God's Timing.* Urichsville, OH: Barbour, 2002.

Printed in the United States
by Baker & Taylor Publisher Services